RAISING A PARENT

Riscardo Alvarado

In order to maintain their anonymity, in some instances I have changed the names of individuals and places. I have also changed some identifying characteristics and details such as physical properties, occupations and places of residence. These changes were made to protect the privacy of individuals. I have tried to recreate my memories of events and locales, as well as conversations with my mother.

RAISING A PARENT Copyright © 2020 by Riscardo Alvarado
Author: Riscardo Alvarado
Editing: Gerianne F. Scott/EmmaJanePress
Assistant to Ms. Scott: Judy Baldaccini
Proofreading: Maxene Kupperman Guiñals
Proofreading of Chancletas y Chancletazos: Dorcas Greene
Technical Assistant: Steve Morales
Design & Layout: CreativeDetails.net
Photo Credits
Front Cover: Issac Diggs
Inside Family Photos: Alberto Morales, Jr.
Photo of Author: Melvin Wright
Back Cover photo of Foforito: Riscardo Alvarado
ISBN # 978-0-578-75215-0

DEDICATION

———

Affectionately dedicated
to the memory of Foforito y Chuito
(Beatriz Berrios Morales & Juan De Jesus Alvarado)

I LOVE ALL YOU GUYS

———◆———

I would like to acknowledge ALL the generous spirits—too many to print—and fearful that my memory could lapse during the roll call. It's with a tremendous sense of gratitude that I embrace your honest criticism and your words of encouragement that fueled me forward. Therefore... Blessings to all...

Un abrazo,
Riscardo

WHAT'S IN A NAME?

My mother misspelled Richard on my birth certificate. I misspelled Fosforito in my journal. In each case, the original intents were bland. The errors have morphed into poetic license. So, I became Riscardo and my mother became Foforito. To date, these are embraceable mutations of misspellings.

Globally, nicknames and terms of endearment are used to address someone and or to refer to them. My mother's first name was Beatriz; her nickname was Foforito. Throughout this memoir, I refer to my mother with the following terms: la vieja, mi mamita, my moms, my honey, my sugar, my girl, my lady,... and a few more. The appropriate capitalization is used whenever the term is a direct address to her. The terms on these pages are never presented as disrespectful or belittling. Between us they were always appropriate and... endearing.

✦

CONTENTS

Translations of Spanish words and phrases located in Appendix under the Glossary in the back of the book.

PROLOGUE

———◆———

THIS DARK NIGHT AWAKENS the solitude that smothers my sense of independence. A round lamp full of itself directs me to a lonesome place of my own making; has me on edge. The slippers have scampered to unfamiliar niches as a search party of toes scouts their whereabouts. A room full of carefully placed objects collects dust and thrusts the past onto a lap longing to relive what at present is unattainable. My cupped hands receive a wave of warm water that splashes me to attention; the rest of me, becoming envious, forces me to fully shower. A radio station plays piercing ballads that rummage my memory, causing one eye to squint and tear, as the other clings shut in false bravado. I never manage to towel myself waterless, so the bedcovers collect the last shower drops. I revisit pillows that have willfully embraced my nightly thoughts without question or judgment. I've entrusted in them my fears, secrets, and desires. They have cushioned eager hips ready to burst with pleasure, and muffled sounds that seek a stage for delightful expression. A lavender scent fills my nostrils. I wrangle with my comforter which is unable to provide the consolation I presently seek. The wooden shades splinter a morning light that is bursting with enthusiasm. Dissected rays of sunshine enable me with their pull. Reluctantly, I review my routine (mind you,

1

my routine is not to have a routine), and the to-do list which never seems to shrivel—*my penis should be so lucky.*

I don't know how or where to start. All I know is, I have a story to tell. Last year (2013), Foforito (my mother) passed away. Chuito (my father, Foforito's beloved husband) had made his transition into death over three decades prior.

Scattered, yellow legal pads contain my memories, opinions, emotions. As I poke away at the keyboard, transcribing scribbled notes and details, the chair that should be supporting me is conversation-worthy, but painfully uncomfortable.

So, I guess the beginning would be a good birthing place for reporting the journey of my life while I was caretaker to my mother. I feel a sense of urgency to fulfill this task of sharing before my back gives way.

INTRUSION

MY FATHER'S PASSING came as no surprise. He had reluctantly agreed to relocate to West Covina, with my brother Al and his wife (at the time) Rosie, mostly to please my mother. I had traveled with my parents to assist them with their cross-country move. As per my mother's architectural directions I converted Al's garage into living space for her and my father, only to have him turn up his toes (figuratively speaking, since he was a double amputee).

Leaving my parents in Los Angeles consumed me with the clutter of uncertainty, especially about my dad. Affectionately called Chuito, he was so cool that he couldn't wrinkle linen, and, as a lifelong presser of clothing, he could smooth out wrinkles instantly in the event they occurred. His sense of humor, wit, and uncanny storytelling talents tickled my memory even three-plus decades later.

As I had packed my bags, I knew in my gut I would never see my father alive again. That thought devastated me. I made my way to his wheelchair under the shaded tree, a place where he and his feathered friends congregated. An avid bird lover, he attracted them; in turn, they would sing their songs to him as a reward for his reverence. His eyes welled up... and mine. Cheek to cheek our tears crisscrossed. By all accounts a mangled mess of sentiments.

It was only the second time I had seen my father cry—the first was when his mother, Eugenia, transitioned into death at the age of eighty-four. I recalled that an elder uncle, once lectured to me the machismo ideology that males don't cry. I was a child, navigating my emotions. Chuito came to my rescue, reminding my uncle of whose child I was. My dad became my hero, the one I would always turn to for advice. "As men," he had said, "we are ultimately defined by the tears we share." His profound statement will be revisited as this story evolves. Now my Chuito had become a shell, whittled away by the demons of diabetes which claimed both his legs to the kneecap, and stole his ability to see in his waning days. His reward as a battling warrior was remaining whole on the inside.

A vacuum within a vacuum, I flew home sadly. The cloud formations I saw from the portal rescued me into remembering Chuito's storytelling. I remembered while sitting with him in conversation, a call interrupted his spiel. I sprung from my chair in a huff, rattled the table and spilled my coffee. I snatched the phone, "Wrong number!" Fussing and cursing, I slammed the phone down almost dislodging it from the wall. Chuito calmly pointed to an empty chair and with a commanding presence stated, "Look, he's laughing at you." I chuckled. "There's no one there."

With a more forceful voice he interjected; he needed to state his case. "It's the devil, you allowed him to entertain your focus, I didn't finish my story. Clean up the mess and pour yourself another cup of coffee." He then told a humorous tale of his endeavors. Once done, our belly laughter filled the kitchen. I got up to leave, and Chuito pointed to the empty chair. "Look he's pissed off 'cause he couldn't mess with you. Never forget he's in that chair waiting to pounce. Don't give him your audience."

As the plane landed, that lesson resonated then and resonates still. It was a life-altering moment that I reference religiously. Three months to the day I left Los Angeles, word came of Chuito's passing. I filled the shot glasses we used for entertaining from time to time and dusted off and spun the vinyl music he had introduced me to. One shot down. I allowed myself to be hypnotized as the bulb shedding light on the record grooves caused a surreal presentation of flashing images going 'round and 'round... a carousel. I poured the next shot for Chuito, on the road he could now travel without restrictions. He had suffered much in the last chapters of his life. Marinating in both grief and relief, I was numb for a good while. My emotions were stuck on pause. Suddenly, I realized I had given him all the tears I owned when we parted under th tree three months ago. My thoughts rambled... *we ent this world, without consent, time becomes our value ally... over time, by inheritance or neglect, unwante afflictions incarcerate our will, and inevitability triumph. we descend, time morphs into enemy...*

Probably predicting that he would not be around care for Foforito when she needed him to be, Chuito verbal wishes actually appointed my brother, Al and m as our mother's guardians. Over the next nearly thre decades, Al and I were custodians of our mother's wel being and handlers of her affairs. That task would dera our outlooks and personal aspirations. The running joke between the two us was that we had "joint custody" of our mother. (Our half-brothers, Raymond and Junior, were never part of any responsibility related to my mother's care, although she had raised them in our household. Foforito was always "Titi" to them, because their own mother, Maria remained involved in their lives.) With the assistance of Rosie and Denise, our wives at the time, Al and I galvanized as family and keepers of tradition, on a West Coast to East Coast schedule of residence for our mother.

And then Al's family dynamics changed when he separated from Rosie and formed a new blended family with Yolanda, her children and her grandchildren. For a while Foforito remained living with Rosie and then moved into the new digs Al had established with Yolanda. Having been Queen Bee for such an extended period with Al and Rosie, Foforito was reluctant to share the stage with Yolanda and her children. My mother had to be in control of her environment, or all hell broke loose. The hijinks she performed would later partly be excused as dementia. But at the time Al and Yolanda had been forced to shield their children from Foforito's unsettling accusations of theft. Those assaults created the tense environment that caused Al to alter the details of the joint-custody duties he and I had inherited.

Simultaneously, Foforito decided she no longer wanted to live in California and requested to come live with me on the East Coast. I respected that my brother had taken a stance by defending his sanctuary and those who inhabited it. More importantly, I admired his grounded view as guardian of the family he nurtured and protected. Quite frankly, I envied my brother's cojones for sticking to his decisions. Without careful consideration I accepted Foforito's petition. Thus, my mama landed in my lap. Let me be clear about it, I do not endorse this script for any parent/child relationship. Wedged between cramping my style and feeling privileged to have the opportunity to care for my mother had me at odds, and a tad resentful. Caso cerrado.

First one in, last one out. *The jagged edges of the construction site.* In the dead of winter, standing and/or kneeling on frozen concrete slabs, defines the when and where of my workday... yeah, first one in, last one out... With marking tools in hand, it was my responsibility to transfer the blueprint instructions onto the concrete slabs. Following that, I orchestrated—and dug in with—a crew of carpenters to build from the ground up. In winter relentless wind off the river served as frigid overseer. In the summer stifling heat and humidity become the taskmaster. I had poured thirty years of my life into the brutal world of construction. That fact of life scared me about the health of my remaining years, due to my long-term exposure in mostly toxic and severe environments. Hearing loss, back pains and arthritic bones that constantly chatter are the evidence that war had been waged. After I retired, four months of inactivity had erased thirty years of calluses, garnered mainly in my palms. A hardened grip of a 22-ounce hammer, with its recoil reverberating up my arm, had been replaced by a pen eager to help me revive a dulling memory for the sharing of this story. The obvious battle scars had healed. What caused me most concern was the internal damage not visible to the human eye. I felt convinced that had I remained in the construction trenches I would not have survived to do this writing. Early retirement was a no-brainer.

Somehow my change of lifestyle had forced me, of all things, to re-evaluate my eating patterns. A fleeting glance captured a mirrored image of my emerging belly and receding hairline, coincidently accompanied by many replacement parts—from hearing aids and tooth implants to eyeglasses—not a pretty picture. Arthritic ointments and memory herbs became but a few additions on a growing list included in my basic toiletries. To combat frustrated mirror-glancing, I searched for photos of my youthful chiseled six-pack physique, even though some of the pictures had never been fully developed and many, like the six-pack had been misplaced. Those few pictures I was able to find had given birth to my thoughts of retirement. It had been an opportunity for me to invest thought into what I wanted to do with the rest of my life after I stopped punching the clock. This was a question I tried to answer truthfully, so as not to fool myself out of whatever time I had left.

Eighty-nine years of struggle were permanently wrinkled and tattooed into my mother's facial expressions. I observed her becoming frustrated. Vain, independent, and now frazzled, this woman was having a difficult time adjusting to her age, and the restraints attached to it. I found myself coming to her aid after a failed attempt to reach the bathroom quickly enough. I started removing her bloomers, which I'd always likened to parachutes, as they loitered on the floor shackled around her ankles. Carefully I lifted one limb then the other, so as not to smudge her railed legs. Luckily, those parachutes captured all her mushy feces. Her shanks were a sagging mass of skin hugging unsteady, tired bones. Close to eighty of those eighty-nine years had been spent pedaling sewing machines; once-tight muscles were now softened and fragile to the touch. At the moment, I didn't know how much longer I was going to have to argue with her about wearing adult diapers.

Half-heartedly, Foforito complained about not having a daughter's care to assist her. My father had only produced male genes, six in total. I jokingly mentioned that maybe I should paint my lips, or wear a wig, just to make her feel more comfortable. Not really, I had never been a wig guy. "Hey Ma, what the hell, it's only shit. Relax!" She was fresh out of clean panties, all of them sanitary white. Foforito ran through them—no pun intended.

"Come on, Vieja[2]," I summoned her with the term of endearment, as I presented a Depends. Reluctantly, she submitted and accepted the adult disposable underwear, which we caretakers frequently called "Pampers" regardless of the particular brand of the moment; thus, reinforcing the resistance of prideful and embarrassed elders. Under her breath, she mumbled (like my favorite cartoon character, Popeye), "Pampers." Once again confronted with caretaking role reversals, I offered her a treat for her false sweet tooth. Then I put her to bed with a pat on her backside. She turned and flashed me that, "Don't do that shit to me" look. But I also saw the smile behind the smirk. Softly she complained of a pain on the side of her face and wanted to get it checked out. I noted that as an urgent request, because

Foforito detested doctors and hospitals. I tucked her into bed, with "La bendición."

"Que Diós te bendiga," brought the day to its close.

———

Dressing Foforito for her doctor's visit, I couldn't help but reminisce about Puerto Rican goodbyes. All those years ago, the finale of every weekend's events on the social calendar was exactly the same. The only thing that changed was the location of the gatherings. The same music, food, and drunken conversations would resurface in a different home each week. Our parents would dress us up during the winter months. Scarves around our necks, like nooses. I'll never forgive or forget the stigma attached to that vinyl Elmer Fudd hat, with the earmuff implants. We sweated into the night as the adults proceeded to prolong the farewell ritual. Consequently, preparing La Vieja[3] for the elements was payback time. I wrapped a scarf, positioned her wool cap, and forced the gloves on her hands. The coat got zippered up, and I threatened her with a vinyl Elmer Fudd hat to wear, if she removed the one I had chosen for her. I had succumbed to the reality that raising one's parent definitely challenged one's patience. Perseverance became the muscle I most needed to exercise. It was the lesson learned as I began to understand the nature of our moments together.

It turned out that the pain she had been complaining about on the side of her face was a case of Shingles. She was transferred from the clinic visit to the hospital.

I followed the ambulance in my car. In a short time, I entered the emergency room where my mother lay waiting for admission to a bed upstairs. Foforito's fragile condition alarmed me. Drained of energy and spirit, she was listless, like a wilted flower drooping in the heat; unsteady, unsure, and unwilling to accept her frailty.

A three week stay in the hospital, which included one week in ICU, shook the core of Foforito's resolve and left me wobbled. In fact, I called my brother, Al in California to let him know the gravity of the situation and advised him I would keep him updated. Finally, my mother was Shingles-free. *What next?* I guessed that she would require therapy to help her recapture her swing. My suspicion was confirmed by conversations I had with the nurse, who insisted rehabilitation had to be next. Explaining the process to Foforito for her total healing would be difficult; after all, she had been pleading to go home. What convinced her of the inevitable was a failed attempt to reach the bathroom on her own. Her defeated look was evident and disheartening. It became apparent to her and spared me having to defend the necessity of physical therapy. "Muchacho, ésto me tiene debil de verdad." At least for the moment she submitted to the relocation. We were both stunned by her debilitated condition; we were both clueless about rehab.

Fortunately, the social worker guided us through the maze of economic uncertainty, spelling things out in layman's terms. Much to my relief I learned Medicare would be picking up the tab, which became a blessing for me in numerous ways, beginning with timing. What would be my mother's short-term stay in the rehabilitation facility coincided with a long overdue construction being done in my house. It was overwhelming having two separate contractors in the house to replace windows, as well as upgrade an antiquated heating system. So, not having Foforito in the reconstruction dust, danger and confusion was indeed a wonderful thing. Holding on to my sanity was an added bonus.

Unfortunately, the social worker had not prepared us for the population layout of the residence; not that I believe she could have or even should have. On my own I walked down the halls and surveyed the place. The accommodations and patient population was a disturbing mixed-bag. There was no painless way to describe the painful image. A stale condensed atmosphere was apparent, especially in the day room where I saw un-attending attendants. Patients with various abilities and disabilities did not seem to be receiving specific attention according to their needs. Patients who were there as permanent residents, as well as those who were there merely for restorative physical therapy were all lumped together. It felt counter-productive. From a business standpoint, I suppose it was more profitable to house short-term rehabilitation patients than it was to house permanent residents destined to expire there.

Watching both groups I took a deep breath, tried to sort out my feelings and anticipate Foforito's. What would she think about these conditions and the people here—both caretakers and patients? More importantly what was she thinking about her own condition? I supposed each of us, in our own way were wondering if she was being sent to this place to restore her health or to spend her final days.

Co-operation and patience would be basic requirements for her recovery. Ornery and anxious, Foforito never exercised either of these. She would definitely be put to a test that already included, "I hate this food" and mandatory physical therapy. As her agent, facilitator, advocate, son, I was being recruited for the ride.

Living close to the facility allowed me more frequent opportunities to mingle with staff. It also made them aware that my concerned-eye on my mother's care was nearby. The climate was simultaneously challenging and demoralizing. So, as the warriors Foforito and I had come to be we rolled up our sleeves. Foforito despised hospital foods, in this case she had taken exception to the menu at the residence. When I observed the bland unattractive plates of food I understood her disdain. In turn, I became my mother's personal chef, cooking for her at least two meals, daily. Occasionally I purchased foods I knew she liked and converted her mealtimes into playful theater. I would arrive with cloth on arm, like a waiter. One particular day I forgot the cloth, so I substituted an adult diaper in its place. She got a big kick out of that. In that moment, watching her crack up, I realized how simple and intense the power of love can be.

That day after eating the bowl of oatmeal I'd gotten to her before the 8 AM breakfast hour, Foforito sounded off in "woe is me" frustration. Her concession speech waved like a white flag in the room. Listening to her doom and gloom complaining, I felt like saying to her, "It's been a good haul. if you want to throw in the towel, so be it." But I didn't. I realized that my mother needed a moment to decide if she was going to allow her struggles with aging to consume her or uplift her. Foforito's will to 'hang in there' was waning; her armor was becoming software. My pep talk was spontaneous and unrehearsed. I told her I would be supportive of whatever decision she made about going forward.

A week later La Vieja began combing her own hair and applying a little face powder, it was evidence that she was determined to reclaim her might. I was pleased and encouraged by her progress. For the first time since she left the hospital and entered the rehab facility we were able to breathe a sigh of optimism. Then we got to work with physical therapy. I stayed in the room alongside Foforito and the therapist during PT sessions, both to see how it was done and to support Foforito emotionally, and physically if needed. Observing her hard work, I made it a point to validate Foforito's efforts by complimenting and hugging her. At the same time, I was learning what to do for her when she returned to the prize—the comforts of home. She was enthusiastic about my tales of renovation progress back at my house. Foforito had also made the choice to isolate from the general population. It was understandable that she chose to be non-social in her temporary setting. Her commentary about being "uncomfortable around elderly folks," was as informative as it was amusing. I guess, even at the age of ninety, Foforito still viewed herself as an advanced adult, far from being a helpless elder.

One Saturday morning, when I arrived at the residence, Foforito was coating the daylight with her doom-and-gloom complaints. Dementia had not only introduced itself; it had actually made itself at home. I felt ill-equipped to evict this unwelcomed guest. Foforito's repression and her date of release were that morning's redundant themes. I had prepared a bowl of oatmeal for her and carried it to the rehab residence. The still hot vapors found their way up her nostrils and teased her hungry taste buds. Unfortunately, her opportunity to enjoy her oatmeal was disrupted by her severe hemorrhoid discomfort. Her sphincter strength just wasn't what it used to be, causing her pain and fear for the loss of muscle tone in her rectum. Prompted by her need to be guarded and cautious on her unstable travels to the bathroom led my mother to warn me against becoming old. Thoroughly dissatisfied with her latest disability, she acknowledged her ascent into the ranks of the elderly.

Over the twenty-five years after our father's death, while Al and I had shared joint custody of our mother, I came to recognize one constant in Foforito's behavior: fussing about something was her staple and her norm. My father was a saint. He accepted my mother's complaints as a way of life; not as a burden. Personally, I didn't aspire to sainthood. So, sometimes I had to step outside myself, exhale, and simply reassess the moment's pressures and uncertainties. I had no blueprint for this; I didn't even realize yet our reality had a title... and rules. Things weren't always spelled out in black and white.

While I rustled up some dinner that same evening, I already knew Foforito never met a diet she liked, approved of, or followed. "I'll eat what I want till the day I die," she stated, even if her choices tortured her. It mattered little to her that I, too, suffered the brunt of those consequences. As long as the refrigerator stocked ketchup, mayo, mustard, and more; the medicine cabinet had to be armed with over-the-counter remedies for her indiscretions. In other words,

Mylanta, Pepto Bismol (cherry flavored), Preparation H, and IMODIUM® A-D always had to be available in-house. I guess when you reach a certain age you can abandon responsibility for your actions. Such was entitlement earned for having survived long enough to be revered by those in your circle... and beyond.

Foforito was in punishing discomfort. My immediate mission was to help her become comfortable. Moment by moment I was learning that the aging process for elders brought unpredictable health challenges to the body, the mind and/or the soul; sometimes at the same time, sometimes one right after the other. At least that was the case with this elder, my mother. The hardest part was figuring out what was wrong, and how to help because some challenges were visible, while others were hidden, even unknown... yet. Predictability was a critical part of preparing the fix. So far, my mother had been diagnosed with weakened sphincter muscles (the supporting muscles to her rectum) which would cause her uterus to slip. We had been advised by her primary care doctor that given her age and in her present state, a surgical procedure was out of the question. We had an idea of what was coming, we didn't know what was coming with it; and we had no fix.

Foforito was in punishing discomfort. Advocating on her behalf I presented the situation to the attending nurse. She said she was aware of my mother's condition, however, reinserting the fallen uterus would not be done by her and not likely happen on her watch. She told me that she had left a message for the doctor. He would return possibly Monday, making Tuesday the more likely day he would see her. That said, the attending nurse dismissed me like the soiled diapers which were routinely cast into the trash bins. It seemed to me that the attending nurse was disinterested in handling my mother's immediate needs.

Instead, her priority became dispensing medications, especially the nightcap sedative which rendered the residents easier for the nighttime staff to handle during their "babysitting" duties. The attending nurse's lack of compassion annoyed me the most. My hurting heart was percolating rage and preparing angry words for my mouth.

I recalled what my father had always told me, "Don't entertain irresponsible energy, it's more dangerous than the negative one. Deflect it, or just give it back." So, as tactfully as possible, I asked that nurse if she would allow me to stick my hand up her anal cavity and rip out her secure uterus? And would she then wait patiently for a doctor to perhaps stop by after the weekend to review that unsightly situation?

Twenty minutes later an ambulance arrived to take my mother to the ER. She spent four days at Christ's Hospital mainly for treatment of a urinary tract infection as I was quickly learning the impact of the hidden on the visible and vice versus. Antibiotics, observation and precaution was the course of action at the hospital. But, I knew the prescription for antibiotics would soon end and regardless, antibiotics do not repair weak sphincter muscles and a fallen uterus. Then the miracle happened... A specialist here at Christ's Hospital advised us that there was a procedure available to remedy my mother's problem and that he personally would perform the surgery. He later performed that operation to repair my mother's sphincter muscles and as promised did not put her in harm's way during the process. But first, since the progress made in therapy had been set back, return to the residence was mandatory. I felt as if I was shoveling sand into the ocean. At least the specialist had handed me a bigger shovel to work with.

Although nearly deaf after spending the bulk of her life in a sweatshop environment, my mother rejected the necessity of getting hearing aids. At times, her inability to hear well made for convoluted dialogue. I was relieved that she understood that this rehab stay would be a short one, as long as she did her part. Again, I made it a point to be present at her therapy sessions, so I could have a firsthand account of her follow-up exercises for recovery. If there was one thing I wanted to inherit from her, it was her spunk. The fire in her warmed my heart, even if it at times it burned up my resolve. People naturally gravitated to her; her therapist was no exception. A "joy" was the word that he used to sum up her will to move forward. In turn, I welcomed the professionalism from him and his coworkers who jointly advanced my mother's recovery. Nonetheless I was sympathetic to his plight as a therapist in such a compromised environment.

Firsthand, I witnessed those in therapy in that apathetic atmosphere. Blanketed with incoherence and defeat, bodies lay dormant in scattered heaps. Many patients had been sedated; cast aside. Dare I say ditched? Sandwiched between the dayroom population, caretakers wore helpless expressions as they moved through a brittle decay of humanity who were wasting away, unresponsive to their once healthier mind's will. A lady, also visiting moved about uneasily. Small chatter with her brought to surface some guilt-ridden feelings. I'm glad I had the moment to listen as she referred to the broken jalopies we become over time. For a minute we are in a garage, I met her at the metaphor and mentioned the importance of oil changes. Perhaps she was viewing the future image of self, as I had contemplated my own on many occasions. That autumn day had lost its daylight, diminishing everyone's outlook. On the untuned piano in the corner of the dayroom, only dust was playing a sad song which all of us were humming on some level. I needed to get my mother home for her sake, as well as for my own.

There were things to be done between my mother's discharge from the rehab facility and her homecoming. I needed a couple of days to revamp the space to accommodate her and her present issues. I also needed to prepare myself emotionally for becoming a full-time caretaker. On the day my mama was released from the rehab center, I learned a valuable lesson. Advocating for her benefits would require some bare-knuckle, roll-up-my-sleeves, no-nonsense work. Luckily wearing short sleeves eliminated one aspect of the battle. Attached to her release form was a lengthy list of medications, eight in total. Officially, Foforito was scheduled to become a prescription junkie. My mother had no prescription plan on record. The pharmacist made me aware that $512.00 bill was due to be paid upon receipt; we were ill-equipped to tackle that digit. The old Chinese cliché, "No ticky, no shirty," came to mind as I pondered my next move. An argument would likely fall on deaf ears, but what the heck? So, I presented the thick-headed question. "What happens if she can't pay for these medications?"

There was a silent pause from the other end of the line. Maybe he was searching for a sympathetic response, a dignified alternate solution; dare I hope? Then came the chilling retort which made me wince. "I don't know what to tell you. Will that be all?" In the question of life and death, it seemed money was dictating her fate. That moment left me bowed yet hardened. I looked into the phone repulsed by the pharmacist's attitude, yet appreciative for the news he had honestly told me. It gave me a literal understanding of what was meant by "a tough pill to swallow."

I started reviewing all her cocktails for wellness. I took the liberty of calling her primary doctor who had prescribed all those drugs. I'd never met a doctor who had good penmanship, so I asked him to tell me the names of the prescriptions and to spell out their uses in layman's terms. He told me that the first pill was to improve her appetite. At the time I couldn't feed her quickly enough! One down. Another was for high blood pressure; her pressure was normal. The nurse's review alerted me that had she taken that medication it would have landed her back in the hospital. Two down. One more was for sugar imbalance. Her tests had proven she was not pre-diabetic, much less diabetic. In the end, only aspirins were purchased, more so for the headache I had inherited from the incompetence by design, of the prescription medication regime. It was a learning curve which allowed me to better understand the nature of the beast. Being inquisitive can be a wonderful tool we should always exercise. A great side-effect of my investigation was that I would be able to avoid pill dispensing wrestling sessions with my mom. She always complained, "They do more bad than good. Fuck 'um. I'm not taking them any longer." And my personal favorite, "I feel like a chicken eating corn all day." After she realized I had advocated on her behalf against their use, I became her hero. She put her hand out, "Give me five." She was a trip! As we headed back home I began feeling like the *Driving Miss Daisy* chauffeur. Oddly enough, I was okay with the title.

—————

I spent my fifty-fifth birthday transporting an oak cabinet from my home in New Jersey to a friend's home in New York City. An imposing organizer with sixty-eight compartments, ideal for storing supplies for my arts and crafts endeavors, I had grown quite attached to this piece of furniture. Even while lifting onto my pick-up truck the wooden beauty which I had stripped and restored to its present usefulness, I had an ongoing internal argument about selling the cabinet and facilitating its removal from my home. In order to tend to my mother, my organizer cabinet was a casualty. It was just too bulky for the space I had designated for her recovery. Under normal circumstances, turning fifty-five and retiring from the Carpenters' Union would have been cause for major celebration. The new circumstances demanded that all parties or festivity-related activities were to be put on hold indefinitely. They became nonfactors on the priority list. In order that Foforito would not have to trek up and down steps, I got my friend, Yogui, to assist me in transporting an ottoman downstairs. It turned out that Foforito refused to sleep downstairs, claiming that she felt detached. Besides, she wanted to use going up and down the steps for exercise. I guess it was Foforito just being Foforito. In retrospect, I understood her need to have me close by; she felt vulnerable and I was her security blanket. So, I became kind of cool with it, in a reluctant way. Yes, I regretted selling my cabinet.

Organizer. Ottoman. Fifty-five. Happy Birthday.

The first few days of the new arrangements presented challenges involving process and communication. They were like the first few days at the rehab facility. Each of us had expectations; each of us had expectations. As always Foforito was doing much too much—making her bed, hand-squeezing oranges with a spoon, washing dishes, sweeping—exhaustive activities for one in her weak condition. Inserting her brand of humor, she drew the line by refusing to do window washing and mopping. My concern was that she was overexerting herself and would wind up back in the hospital. Of course, she did not see it that way. She wanted to prove—to herself? —to me? —that she could keep up with doing her part. During our breakfast coffee conversations, I suggested that she relax a little and use the time to make vacation plans for some time in the near future. Would she take the offer as a reward for her efforts? Secretly, I hoped it was an incentive—not that she needed one to get involved—no, I wanted her to slow down. Foforito was in a frail state; a little worn and a lot frustrated. She mumbled, "Why monitor what I eat, or even exercise, or do my part? Que mierda!"

Her defeated tones were 'woe is me' violins blasting in my head. They were wearing me out. Frustration visited mother and son equally those days. I knew I was doing *my* part with her rehabilitation regime. It seemed she didn't appreciate that, and it was *fucking* pissing me off! This would have been the only time in my life when I could have screamed at my mother without fear of her pulling parental rank and giving me a smack. That wasn't going to happen. So many years on industrial sewing machines in the confines of the sweatshops had caused my mother to have serious hearing impairment. Additionally, she refused to get tested or prepped for hearing aids. Even though my vocal cords had been overworked in simple conversations with her, she couldn't hear me. Excuse the pun, but my concerns, even if I screamed them mostly fell on deaf ears. Without malice, I started venting, loudly.

"If you want to die that's fine, I will not condemn your decision, however, under someone else's watch." Then, under my breath I muttered, "Maybe at that rehab residence." Back to loudly again, "I will not entertain defeat under this here roof." I caught myself. She lifted her face and her eyes were wet with understanding. Finally, she was showing a half-hearted attempt to consider my argument. Raising my voice in these explosive tête-à-têtes was taking its toll. My vocal cords and my patience were stretched to their limits.

Foforito couldn't fathom why her body wasn't responding to her demands. "When did I become so weak?" was written on her face. Like wind-blown pages of an open book, our morning coffee chats started filling the unlined sheets of a memoir in the making. My father, Chuito, had been the one person who had been able to talk sense to Foforito which she understood. I used his example of resiliency to fuel her forward. I also used her example as a caretaker for Chuito to highlight what I expected from her for her own recovery.

Role reversal for Foforito was unfamiliar and uneasy. It was especially difficult to digest since she had no daughters who could tend to her private-parts' moments. Wounded pride wasn't a good recipe for recovery. Making light of the gravity I shared, "You rubbed my back, I'll rub yours. You wiped my butt, I'll wipe yours; after all, one good wipe deserves another." I started massaging her back, tender and aching from inactivity. Her thinning white hair, unkempt, began shedding, graced the pillow. Her moans, half pain, half pleasure, filled the room's silence. Her bra's imprint still reddened and invasive on her wrinkled back slowly evaporated with my gentle strokes. Against my palms, I could count the ribs on her skeletal frame; so brittle. Her delicate back coated only by scarred flesh, hazed by a backwardly abusive mother, who no doubt had mimicked her own mishandled and abused past. The scars were telling like a book written in Braille. Reading the stories with my fingers, they collaborated our conversations, which always reeked of unresolved resentment.

Her mother, Doña Provi's beatings were legendary. Perhaps, that's why I never really embraced her when she came to live with us. It saddened me to think that I never called her Abuela. She was always kind to me, but she was always Doña Provi. I had never met the person described to me by my mother. I guess by the time Doña Provi was interacting with my generation she had mellowed. People do mellow with time.

Foforito's frame was hungry for her mate's embrace. Chuito had been the only man who ever loved and understood the fire in her. Her gentle husband comforted, defended, caressed, and truly loved her, until the day he died. I placed a sheet over her body as she eased into a sleep. Then I slipped away, gingerly stumbling up the treads, with what felt like her life's struggles in my hands. The weight slumped my shoulders into the posture of the overworked. I needed to be rid of the accumulated baggage I had collected it seemed overnight. Finally, sitting at my desk looking at my parents' wedding picture, a tidal wave of stored emotions escaped me, liberated me. I prayed for the two single most important people in my life. One departed and the other struggling... in wait.

The weeks that followed were a slow, grinding adventure. Instantly, I had to become nutritionist to an eighty-nine year old, who was hell-bent on satisfying all her cravings. I welcomed her ravenous appetite as a means of building up her strength; the downside was that her choices were starting to wreak havoc with her digestive track. Her workouts, on the other hand were playful. I had no gauge for what was enough, so I allowed her to dictate what was sufficient. "If Pop could only see you now," I teased as she started her leg lift exercises. She chuckled at the thought of what he would say. The old man was very witty. I sensed she had been faking body pain to get rubdowns. Little did she know all she needed to do was ask.

One thing I learned over the years, Foforito was a master manipulator. Call it controlling, meddlesome, conniving... she worked it to suit her needs. She basked in the undivided attention. The "Ay, bendito" look had become her morning mask. The relationship was altering my life in so many ways. By all accounts it was a strange, and at times bizarre, learning curve. Over time I was able to get a handle simply by having others fill in the voids.

It amazed me how Foforito became transformed when others took time out from their lives just to share moments with her. Particularly welcome were those who had pampering skills. Whenever company arrived, the "Convalescing Sister" act sprang to life. She was engaged and entertained; she thrived on the love juices people offered as a form of concern. I made a concerted effort to recruit family and friends under the pretext of lifting her spirits. It was also a way of allowing myself much needed alone time to assess the matters at hand. Having company was a win-win.

Love was a tremendous healer, especially when it was given with a little glitter and trimmings. Olga, my out-of-pocket home attendant, cut Foforito's hair and managed—surprisingly without difficulty—to care for and tend to those unsightly, petrified toes. Not that my mother wore any open-toed shoes, mind you. Toes seen or unseen didn't change the fact that Foforito was a vain, nearly nonagenarian woman, whose major concern was her appearance. So, Olga's simple acts of kindness were miracles that touched Foforito with heartfelt gratitude; and fueled my days with promise.

The health care system was a complicated maze. Now in home, my mother's visiting nurse was sympathetic and informative regarding the way the system was set up. Holding my hand, she advised me of the guidelines and helped me navigate the labyrinth of bureaucratic bullshit.

"Don't be discouraged... learn to steer the system...," was her prescription for attaining the much-needed benefits.

Watching Michael Moore's movie, *Sicko* had made me feel intimidated. Additionally, after following the visiting nurse's pep talk and private-eye approach, I became downright angry. Had my mother been living independently on her own all those years, she would have become a ward of the state. The tab would have been for room and board, health care: the works. My short visits to the residence had allowed me to view senior drug abuse firsthand. She probably also would have been a 'Prescription Popping Mama.'

As a habit every morning I sat down with my coffee. Reading in between the lines of my daily newspaper always provided me with a chuckle. One headline had the "eulogy" of a manager leaving the New York Yankees while turning down a cool five million dollars. Meanwhile, another ballplayer turned down two hundred million. How ironic, huh? I tried to digest the dollar and nonsense gossip, which was making me nauseous and cynical. I realized that in order to get her a home attendant from the social service programs, my mother would have to liquidate all her assets and lower her monthly Social Security check by a few bucks. I fantasized that afterwards she would probably be shaken by her ankles and strip-searched. At some point, she might have to slide under the limbo pole... leap from a tall building... I would draw the line at a cavity frisk. Something was definitely wrong with this social health- care picture.

My mother had worked too hard for too long, just to be ripped off by the very unions which were supposed to represent her. From one sweatshop to another she had been deprived of so many rights all of her life. Was she now to be humiliated by a corrupt and self-serving system? That would be an abomination! The benefits which were trickling down had me flabbergasted. How shamefully the system went about 'rewarding' the elderly for their honest, hard work was lost on me.

Although the nurse had made me aware that a physical therapist would be provided on a temporary basis, the knock on the door stunned me. Frank, the therapist, had the appearance of a traveling salesman for vacuum cleaners. He had to be at least eighty, but his movement was brisk and full of pep. Astute, but somewhat quirky as he announced himself, I could tell he enjoyed his occupation. The first thing we had to do was fill in all the blanks. The paperwork drove me up a wall. Was it too much to think that within the same agency, they should communicate the client's name, rank, and serial numbers from one department to another? The redundancy of information always got in the way of progress for me. I surmised they were looking for slip-ups to prolong the process, or worse, reject people outright.

Once the paperwork was completed, Frank and I became engaged in conversation. Frank, full of spunk for his age, was interesting and entertaining. He had found an ear at attention that allowed him a platform for expression. Travel, movies, art, and of course, his boxing exploits in the Navy were subjects broached on that initial visit. He even had photographs on hand to validate his life's adventures. Years later I would swear that the animated movie, Up, captured him perfectly. Our lengthy conversation turned out to be more therapy for me than for my mom, his assigned patient. It also allowed me to grasp how socially dysfunctional I had become due to the isolation my new commitments had caused.

Shifting his attention to my mother, Frank offered her the exercise of dance. He took her hand and lead by example. This gesture got him off on the wrong foot with her, since, even when she was feeling better, dancing wasn't her strong suit. On a personal note that troubled me, because at the time I couldn't remember the last time I myself had been on the dance floor. Me, who had always enjoyed dancing!

We proceeded to review a series of exercises for Foforito's recovery. She found Frank to be totally obnoxious; humored him briefly, then dismissed him. Upon his exit she berated the poor guy's, efforts as rubbish. I, on the other hand, found his attempts commendable; after all, he had remained a productive human being well into his eighties and in this single visit he succeeded in conversing me out of my caretaker's funk.

As Frank remained assigned to see my mother, I actually looked forward to his sessions with Foforito. She continued acting out whenever he came by. I'd learned not to make excuses for others' actions, and that included my mother's. Even though I became embarrassed by her naughty behavior, I couldn't ring her ear in punishment, but I did entertain that admonishment, especially when she misbehaved during Frank's visits. She was dead set to not cooperate. I told her if she wanted to be Frank-free she would have to show all parties involved that her recovery was complete.

That incentive fueled her cooperation and lessened her dependence on me as she started exercising independently. The morning sweeps with the broom, washing dishes, squeezing oranges with a spoon were all activities that helped round her into shape.

Losing Frank's services became a casualty of Foforito's recuperation. I missed the lengthy conversations with the quirky therapist. Folks who have been around the block have so much to offer and tapping into his past had been healing for me. Frank and I hugged on his last visit, and he commended me for staying the course with my partner in crime. I didn't seek validation, but it was nice to hear from time to time.

Mary, the visiting nurse, was very encouraged by my mother's speed of recovery. The exercises Frank had entrusted me to administer were part of that reclamation project. A short, plump woman, Mary was a hands-on, no-nonsense professional. It made for a stress-free environment. I admire folks who actually take pride in what they do for a living. Mary's being a female also went a long way. As La Vieja made the sisterhood connection, a vital element, she speeded the process along by cooperating fully. Mary helped me identify the agencies I needed to navigate on the pilgrimage. I was in unchartered waters and greatly appreciated her generous insight. Mom's monthly SSI check barely covered her expenses, which allowed her to receive Medicaid. With study and practice I became empowered to better deal with the bureaucracy, and the potholes set up to swallow the uninformed, especially the elderly. It was critical to obtain the home attendant and prescription plans that are attached to Medicaid. It was a slow process that had me on the fringes of anxiety. Frank was already in the rearview mirror and now Mary was paying me her last informative visit. I maintain the belief that certain folks are placed in our lives for good reason. Mary made that belief a reality with her disposition. In parting, she appointed me the guardian of my mother's uncertain path. Up until then, Mary had made the many twists, curves, and bends manageable with her kindness.

As soon as Mary walked out the door I felt isolated. Her parting hug, genuine, warm, and honest, clung to me as she faded from sight. Even though she left me well-armed, I felt naked and unwieldy, scattered, struggling to understand and perhaps salvage my present. "Suck it up!" kept reverberating in my mind.

I retreated to the pedestal sink to wash away traces of unmanaged sentiments. My cupped hands gathered warm water; the splash awakened angst in me. A battered expression stared back at me from the mirror. It was telling, raw and surreal. I felt deflated and betrayed by the unscheduled assignment. Perhaps most troubling was that there was little joy in what I had chosen to undertake, or rather, what had been thrust upon me. I was becoming a prisoner to duty.

I needed to reverse that view for my sanity's sake; needed to see the silver lining. I laid myself down to rest and map out my plan of attack. Above me the ceiling was murky and uninformative. I was trapped in a web. There were so many loose ends, fragile fragments cluttering my perceived progress. This period of my life could be an opportunity to at least investigate incarcerated issues, now guarded by the macho wardens of my past... Somehow my nap became a launch pad for a spring cleaning of my mind.

All the well-wishers echoed similar themes, repeating like cheap whiskey. After a while, I felt uneasy and intoxicated by their commentaries, including: "Hey, you gotta take care of Moms; you only have one." And, "I know how you feel." I wished people stated the obvious, only to those who needed to hear it, (and left me the hell alone). They should have read my thoughts...

No, you don't have a fucking clue how I feel.

When was the last time you wiped your mother's butt?

What if they replaced those pre-worded, manufactured card remarks with...

"Is there anything that I can do to help?"

"Let me keep her company while you take a breather."

Yeah, that might have worked...

I entertained the bizarre thought of decapitating the next person who asked me how I was doing, without even taking the time to listen to my answer. Was it too much to want a hug? Maybe I should have made up some tee shirts that said, "Spare me the half-ass clichés." A smirk highlighted my unshaved face, as I addressed the situation with my own script...

"Hey, Riscardo, you gotta take care of yourself, you know you only have one you."

"Hey, Riscardo, how you doing?",
"How you holding up?",
"You wanna talk?"

Now, that's more like it... Oh, fuck! Am I starting to go mad here? Or what? It became a light-hearted moment with self as I wiped the remaining shaving cream from my face. It was also at that moment that I seriously decided to keep a daily journal.

Leaving Foforito alone for lengthy periods made me a little paranoid. I needed to run some errands but had to pick my escape moments carefully those days. She had started complaining of an annoying back pain. Sitting up in bed she couldn't wiggle herself flat onto the mattress to the position that alleviated the discomfort of the affliction. I gently wrapped my arms around her. The scent of Johnson and Johnson baby powder filled my nostrils. She draped her fragile limbs like a necklace and adorned my neck with them. Achy and moaning, she cringed. I whispered, "Relax." Those up-close encounters enabled me to better understand the magnitude of what was happening; a welcomed connection, nonetheless, difficult to explain. From left field, a sadness came over me. *Could this be a cruel joke?*

My mind went to years ago, when Denise and I had been unsuccessful after several attempts to become parents. Now, suddenly, I found myself parenting my mother. Like a young child, she depended on me for all her needs. I was finding my way. Immediately, I knew there would never be any reprimand of my wrinkled bundle of joy. She was my mother. *You don't reprimand your mother!*

Before Foforito became a permanent responsibility, Denise and I had become resigned to renting our nieces and nephews from our siblings. Being temp parents was actually pretty cool; the sugar without the toothache, if you will. Denise became an educator, which is being a parent to society, especially by someone as dedicated as she was. On the other hand, without realizing or planning, I had become parent to my mother and her evolving neediness. As I slipped her down onto the bed, a yielding pillow welcomed her. She let out a sigh of relief. In turn, I received a shooting pain that buckled me. Her back, of course, was pain free. *Now what? Was I some sort of a pain conduit?* It was a strange yet interesting occurrence that had me lying next to her perplexed and searching my telephone book for my acupuncturist.

Thanksgiving snuck up on us like turkey farmers on unsuspecting fowl. Foforito always sprang to life when in the borders of a kitchen, especially during the holiday seasons. Thanksgiving wore away at me, as it jumpstarted the Christmas feeding frenzy. Despite my holiday hypocrisy, I was thankful. We rustled up a meal worthy of the occasion, and the turkey was spared its execution.

All the well-intended invitations became a moot point, since Foforito was not up to travel. At the time, taking her outside into the dampness of that grey-coated day was not a good idea. I felt like an overprotective parent. But the truth of the matter was that the weather had us both retreating in cocoon mode.

I took a peek at the barren garden; it was colorless and ashy. When I dared to step out into it, a wintry chill started playing my arthritic bones like a xylophone. Winter could be so dreary, even with a page-turning book in hand. Over the summer months, the wisteria had run amok, wrapping itself like a snake around branches, gates, and fences, vandalizing as it choked all in its path. I felt caught up in its misleading embrace.

My mother's frailty had her frightened of being left alone. The minute I wanted to step out, perhaps to rendez-vous with someone, she went into underprivileged mode, which quite frankly irritated me to no end. Her look was telling and needy. I popped a video into the DVD player until she slid into a snoring slumber. Shit, I could even hear her when I turned off my hearing aids. I couldn't help laughing.

When the phone rang with my brother Al calling to chat—as we often did—one of the things I sensed was that over time he had become more detached with respect to our mother. His calls were generalities. We spoke sports and insignificant... "matters of consequence...", as said in *The Little Prince*. During the period in which Foforito was hospitalized, she seemed to be an afterthought in Al's conversations. I felt adrift; however, I recognized that Al was fed up with our mother's wrecking-ball antics. He had had his fill of her acting out for attention while stepping on other's toes. I tried not to get into the, 'How you doing?'... 'Don't ask.' conversation.

Then, Al asked if I claimed our mother on my taxes; and if not, could he? This would have been a big no-no since claiming her meant becoming accountable for any debt she might incur, namely hospital bills. At that stage, those were a revolving occurrence as her health was declining. The attached deduction wasn't worth it, financially speaking. Half-jokingly I chimed in, "If you want me to send her westward for the summer, you can claim her that way." The silence on the other end spoke volumes. He finally replied, "I'll get back to you on that one." That had been the conversation that confirmed my inheritance of our mother, lock, stock, and barrel.

Al called back as promised. Try as I might, I hadn't been able to generate an upbeat attitude. I guess he picked up on my deflated tone which led to our planning for him to come east to assist in the caretaking and allow me the opportunity to have some time to get away. Hanging with my brother had always been welcomed, regardless of the circumstances. He offered to come over from California to spend the holidays and allow me some time to revamp my spirit. Clearly, he knew that if something happened to me Foforito would be all his. I welcomed the offer; it would also be an opportunity for us to spend the holidays together. The news of Al's visit put a bounce back into my step. Christmas was always a festive period in our lives: my dad's birthday, the week-long preparations, opening gifts, playing with our cousins, the family in a communal weave; festive. Foforito's Christmas present would be too big to wrap, Al being six feet three inches tall. So, his visit, when it became a reality, was two thumbs up in my book. I made plans to airlift my way to P.R. for a couple of weeks after New Year's, while Al tended to La Vieja.

I dusted off a book of poems I had written which highlighted that period in time in bilingual fashion. The *Spanglish* language we created was a volley between the Latino lingo and the street gringo lingo. "Chancletas y Chancletazos", a poem dedicated to my mother, and that patch of time, was appropriate to recite. I approached a makeshift stage in dramatic fashion. I was a bridge betwixt the native tongue and the inherited English language. Reciting that poem beamed me into a better understanding of the intricate function of family, and the role it played in our lives. Later, in a coffee conversation with Foforito, I proposed reciting and reenacting the poem for her. Those words would create a magical time for both of us. At first, she took out her excuse book, a lengthy one might I add. I countered with resolutions for all her concerns. After some arm-twisting she submitted; I recited; and then we were both dancing (our way) in the kitchen.

Even with limited resources, one of my mother's specialties was rustling up a meal, figuratively, in the time it took to fire up a phosphorous matchstick. At least that's how my Tia Blanca saw it, and on the spot she nicknamed her sister-in-law, "Foforito." Additionally, I crowned her Kitchen Queen. White rice, with fried eggs and a slice of spam or Vienna sausages were the regular daily menus dictated by our economic status during trying times. Anything she touched was flavor-filled; skillfully using condiments was ingrained into her arthritic limbs. To help prepare the meal for Al's arrival, I recruited the usual helping hands to perform the heavy hands-on work. Yogui's wife, Dorothy (I've privately labeled that couple The Huggables), and Pat, my energetic, and warm-hearted adopted sister were eager to assist. The fortunes of friendship knew no bounds. Sharing the course of attack with a crew eager to learn trade secrets, I felt blessed. Dementia hadn't obscured Foforito's kitchen skills; that, too was a blessing.

My mom was razor-sharp with those sacred recipes. We made the sofrito, a special seasoning of which ajicitos, recao, cilantro, onions, garlic, red and green roasted peppers, ground peppercorns, sea salt and two tablespoons of olive oil... and of course, the fresh oregano, were pureed and placed into a bowl. Next, all the preparations were made for the pasteles, an African-inspired dish wrapped in plantain leaf and paper, then boiled. (That involved a long-winded recipe that I am forbidden to disclose.) The arroz con gandules, covered with plantain leaves while cooking, was then adorned with red roasted peppers. Once everything was primed, I tied each pastel individually, as I had been taught how to do at the age of eight. The pasteles were packaged in dozens and then placed in the freezer. Later they would be popped into boiling water for about an hour, the final step before serving. These special treats, kind of Puerto Rican Pop Tarts, would be tasty rewards for the crew who helped put them together. Dessert, for sure, was flan; Foforito's false sweet tooth craved the sugar rush. As I stepped back to watch everyone interacting, I witnessed the pride and joy in my mother's eye. Handkerchief on her head, bandana style, she was in her element. This dinner—minus a boar—would be a dressed-down version of Foforito's historical feasts.

When I was young, the annual walk to the butcher for a whole pig had become a bonding ritual for my father and me. His articulate conversations with folks were always seasoned with humor—he was a people person—a quality I would always try to emulate. Clumsily, up five flights of stairs, we would carry that awkward box that I likened to a coffin. Its weight buckled the kitchen table legs. Foforito, with the bandana sitting on her head like a Cinderella crown and her hardened hands, forged by years of gripping the heavy sharpened knives, pounced on the pig's thick skin. She plunged those utensils like a skilled surgeon. Then she impregnated the incisions with sofrito. Her chunky fingers dug into the pig's cuero (skin), seasoning it with precision. She'd review her work and then stick that poor pig some more. (It became a running joke for me to tell my brother to inform her that the pig was already dead.) Once that prep work was completed, the pig got reinserted into the cardboard casket which was transferred to the bakery to get cooked in their ovens. Those steps were a killer, but it kept us in shape.

The final phase had us returning home in a procession, as the skin on the roasted swine seasoned the barrio air. Ohhh, the fights that would break out over chicharrón; that crispy, delicious skin. Chicharrón had the texture of Bonomo's Turkish Taffy candy. As kids, we used to stash that candy in the ice box and have it to savor for the rest of the year. The pork skin, predictably, was gobbled up in less than a day.

Fast-forward to when Al arrived for the Christmas visit: I knew the specially prepared spread, even without the pig, would take my brother and me back to the good old days. And it did.

Our reminiscing took me to our grandmother, Eugenia, a feisty, unconventional abuela. A barrel-shaped, dead-ringer for a Wizard of Oz Munchkin; she was the best storyteller. She drank wine with dinner and had an occasional shot of brandy for a nightcap. Man, how she loved music... and she could dance! And sometimes, she swore. Her daily duty had been to care for her grandchildren while our parents worked their lives away in the sweatshop camps in Manhattan and the Bronx. Eugenia despised taking pictures and not one image of her has ever been excavated to date. However, next to her altar, she had a picture of her daughter, Rosita, who had died at an early age. The details of that family secret remained a mystery. Upon reflection, I remember that the picture showed an unmistakable likeness between me and Rosita, this dead aunt I had never met. I suspect that the resemblance contributed to Eugenia's fondness towards me.

My favorite moments with my abuela were spontaneous spurts of unbridled pleasure.

Our apartment was decked out with flowered wallpaper, some oversized flower-covered butacas and flower-covered linoleum flooring we all called "carpetas." Our living room was like a botanical garden in fabric. I would occasionally joke that we needed a machete to cut through that artificial jungle. Some evenings, Abuela would place my feet atop her chanclas, hold my hand upright, and hug me into her Pillsbury Doughboy frame until my nose was compressed against her belly. I nearly suffocated on a couple of occasions as we skated on the carpetas. Then she would send me for a glass of ginger ale. After she took a sip and she caught her breath, we resumed our dancing. Her consejos were always on point and there was a 'no-nonsense' approach to her that was admirable. I recall once deliberately wanting to step on a pile of shit because I had heard that legend had it to do so was good luck. Well, she cleared that up in a hurry, "Muchacho, shit is shit. They say that, so you don't feel bad when you step in it." "Abuela, you played the number when you stepped in doo-doo," I replied, recollecting a day she smudged her shoe in some dog crap. She smiled and without a pause whispered, "Just in case, one never knows." And so, with one of her famous quotes, she had gotten the last word on that debate.

Such was my life with Eugenia until I was eleven years old. It was a muggy, listless night as the urban stench emanated from the streets of the Bronx. I took to the fire escape for the drama-filled activity on Washington Avenue. The bodega was sandwiched between the social club and the Pentecostal church; one was always trying to convert the other. The clashing mambo-crazed tambourines in battle with the voices of the do-gooders committed to saving the lost souls were constant entertainment. In the background, PLAP-PLAP-PLAP—PLAP-PLAP!! the clave beat of the congueros and the coro of wanna-be-rumberos competed for attention. Friday night beat-downs were better than some of the Gillette fights on TV and live to boot. I glanced at the window where my grandmother was a perched fixture with a pillow cushioning her massive forearms. She would sit like a short, plump gargoyle camouflaged by curtains or the dark side of night. So many quarters for buying candy had found their way to me as she parachuted them in a number two paper bag out the window, down five flights. Her absence at the window was odd. The stifling heat that night had been all-consuming, so I went to the fridge for a limber, then doubled back to my spot for some stargazing.

Suddenly a racket startled me to attention. Foforito was hysterical; her screams intensified and disturbed my 'I don't want to be bothered' mood. I jumped like a paratrooper onto the carpetas. Al and Tony dashed from their room. We converged in the communal quarters. Huddled with my brothers, I caught a glimpse of Chuito feverishly trying to dress his mother. The beads of sweat had saturated his sleeveless tee shirt. A moist view now obscured the unfolding melodrama as I saw my mountain of joy in a listless state. She had always been the most influential person in my daily life. The animated woman who lit up my sense of adventure with her pastel-colored cuentos was hunched in an incapacitated posture; helpless. How could this be? Chuito fumbled with her slippers. Gently, she took her arthritic hands, which were mangled and muscular and twisted and strong, and she placed them on my father's face as if searching for a lost treasure. She compressed his saddened expression into her bosom, nurturing his sentiments. That moment encapsulated for me the definition of family and respect for our elders, the gatekeepers of culture and traditional values. "No te veo, m'ijo, me voy." A chorus of sobs were on cue as we began to understand the gravity of her languished state. She clung to my dad reinforcing in that embrace that he was a good son, one worthy of her bendiciones.

A cavalry of men scampered up the steps as the social club partygoers arrived to assist Chuito with his mother, Eugenia. The love of my life was placed in a kitchen chair and brought down five flights of stairs by four wobbly, intoxicated brother-friends; clumsily, but in one piece. Little did I know then that it would be the last time I'd ever see her alive. A neighbor called for an ambulance. A long wait ensued as the sands in the hourglass of her life sifted. I guess our part of the hood was a low priority for emergency service. Finally, the sirens announced their arrival as a communal sigh of relief punctuated the air. My grandmother's last moments of revival were extinguished by empty oxygen tanks—props to provide a false sense of security to those clinging to hope. My dad was devastated.

The sleepless night gave way to daybreak. The doorknob turned as Chuito, a reluctant messenger, announced, "Estoy huérfano." His defeated look and quivering lips were so telling of the grave moment pulling at him mercilessly. My mom and my dad held each other up with four rickety knees and two broken hearts. She guided him to the kitchen chair where he collapsed, a shattered son, a newly admitted orphan. I went into my grandmother's room where she endured her last moments and bid her son farewell. The room was dark, a candle flickered on the altar, her unmade bed had housed her last struggle. A ray of light tried unsuccessfully to find its way from the courtyard to touch her trinkets and mementos littered atop the dresser drawers. A bata perfumed by Maja soap draped the bed's corner. Her scent faded as I closed the door, never to reenter her room again. That period became a blur for me.

Al accompanied Chuito spreading the news and making the necessary preparations for Eugenia's funeral services. My first introduction to a wake sickened me literally and figuratively. I became one giant teardrop. I didn't know then that I'd attend way too many wakes in my future, nor that none would be as moving as that one. The crowd of family and well-wishers filled all niches and overflowed the Ortiz Funeral Home to bid my grandmother, "Goodbye."

That was also the beginning of what would become my monthly odyssey to Saint Michael's Cemetery, right across the Triborough Bridge into Queens. I remembered the first trip as if it were yesterday. I was eleven years old when my Abuela died. Forty-four years later I still recalled the anguish captured on my father's face; his love for her was worthy of admiration. Without fail, he fought through any weather and made his way to the gravesite. On his knees, he would recite a rosary and then kiss the cold slab of marble before he proceeded into Pepe Pantoja's car, or the car of any other person recruited to drive him on that monthly pilgrimage. He performed that ritual until he relocated to California, only to be shipped back three months later and slipped into that same patch of earth. I must admit I have been delinquent at times, but I'd never lost my way, fifty-three years and counting. Two-thirds of the plots were spoken for as Chuito joined his mother eighteen years later. I shuddered as I remembered that plot had one more reservation.

One Sunday morning, as was custom, I bundled up my mother, wrestling as usual with the "what to wear?" wardrobe. Finally, she was ready as we prepared for that somber ride to Saint Michael's Cemetery. For our trek, my mother required specific staples. I secured the staples for her: vintage threads and sacred bra, along with her glasses, purse, and scented sandalwood rosary beads, gifted by a lifelong friend, Deleine "Pete" Santiago.

Remembering for two folks was wearing away at my memory. I doubled up on the gingko-biloba. Having done my homework made for a stress-free morning. I learned to be diligent. Over time, Foforito's hard drive had faded, while mine was put to the test. I wrapped her up for her date with old man winter: gloves, scarf, and sweat socks, which kept dropping down on her lean ankles. The drooping socks unsettled her because she had to look her best for Chuito. I jokingly suggested that maybe we should get some long suspenders. The attempted humor didn't go over well. She became combative and became defiant about the wool hat. A short clash ensued; again, I warned her against removing the woolen roof from her head. "You want the Elmer Fudd hat, Ma?" That time she actually found the warning amusing; her choppers popped almost like bread from a toaster. Keeping her healthy was very trying, so I had to draw a line, without compromise. I was worn out from emergency room visits. *Shit! They knew me on a first name basis at Christ Hospital.*

While traveling through the Holland Tunnel and making our way towards Queens, I put up a flawed argument for picking up the tab on the flowers, knowing it put her in a feisty mood. Previously I had slipped a twenty-dollar bill into her wallet for the flowers she always insisted on purchasing. As her banker, I needed to keep most of her money out of her hands, since she hoarded her green in forgettable places. With her impaired memory, she would give me the all-accusing eye. The strain of handling her finances was taxing! Despite her objections, I limited the in-hand funds she could misplace. The crestfallen ride had us two chatterboxes on mute as she scrambled inside her purse on an intensive and private search. Even as she discovered the twenty spot, she was untrusting of her partner in crime. When she paid for the flowers, she chastised the Korean woman about her bloated prices.

At the gravesite, the bush planted some forty years before had mushroomed. Its imposing presence camouflaged the headstone that stood above those that were buried under snow. Its marbled heartiness umbrellaed over the only plot that had Foforito's interest. My mother separated the long-stemmed roses and gently placed them in a heart-shaped manner, symbolic of her and my father's moments together. As if tinkering with a tailored dress, she stepped back to explore her composition until self-satisfaction was attained. The cold had caused her nose to run. While I gently dried it with her handkerchief, there was a little resistance and her teeth began to chatter. Foforito hooked onto my arm as she stepped cautiously and respectfully between the army of stones that stood like soldiers. Her gingerly walk was a reminder of her decline; unstable and therefore guarded.

With my assistance, she scooted into the passenger seat. I turned up the heat to welcome her in from the biting cold that had managed to infiltrate the bones in both of us. Although she appreciated the heat, she was obviously dissatisfied with her limited mobility. Her faraway gaze rummaged through a collection of valuables. I was sure that in her bittersweet treasure trove were precious rewinds of partnership with the man who had graced her world with kindness and witty humor. An unorthodox smile gave way on quivering lips. Tears began to settle in the crevices that time had chiseled into her cheeks. The scented sandalwood rosary beads perfumed the moment. They were tangled around her arthritic fingers, disjointed like a snake in a mangrove. Her cadence resonated even in silence, as she nervously massaged the beads, one by one. A teardrop made its way, past the border of her lip. Perhaps she welcomed the salty taste as a new wave of emotions saturated her wrinkled cheeks. I placed my arm around her fragile frame. She began to wail. In an attempt to lighten the moment, I told her to be mindful of getting boogers on my coat. I offered her my handkerchief and made her aware that it might already house some of those slimy things. (Intimate moments, to be sure.) Foforito provided me a dirty, disapproving stare without interrupting her rhythmic telling of the beads.

I stepped outside the car to offer parting words and provide each of us a moment of privacy. As the pendulum swayed well into the winter of Foforito's decline, dementia had sought quite fittingly to allow a brief period to revisit something deprived to many. My mother had savored love's embraceable moments. Her life with my dad, which provided her a sanctuary to heal from years of backhanded abuse, had liberated her from past pains. Chuito meant the world to her; his absence clawed away at an unbridgeable void. Soulmates are hard to come by.

What I found most troubling was how Foforito had done everything humanly possible to undo her children's attempts to replicate those precious sentiments she had shared with my dad. Conveniently, she had sabotaged our relationships with our chosen mates. I suspect lifelong insecurities played a major role in those affronts. Simply put, our companions became collateral damage. *Did Foforito want to shield us from the pain that was her terrible company?* Was she a visionary, or was she just controlling her own personal interests? The hush echoed past wishes for wisdom, patience and blessings, which had always been given without reservation from my dad.

With my *Driving Miss Daisy* hat in place, I assumed my position as chauffeur. Turning the steering wheel, I glanced around at the condition of St. Michael's Cemetery. Some areas showed that it had been established in the mid-1800s, over a century before I was born. I saw the roots of cypress trees planted for beauty, pushing through the black-top asphalt that had been laid to upgrade the cemetery roads. Crumbling pieces of the broken pavement scattered to announce our departure and confirm my sad assessment of the disrepair. Slowly turning her head Foforito strained for a final view, as if she saw something no one else could see.

The road that led to the exit gate was long and practically abandoned. Respecting the potential damage that the icy gravel could do to my car, I drove slowly. Foforito had finished saying her rosary and was staring straight ahead. Peripheral glances at the procession of headstones on both sides of the path caused me to reflect. With one space left in the family plot and my mother one step closer to the other side of midnight, I needed to know what her final wishes were. Broaching the subject provoked a cynical response. "Shit! No estoy fria y ya me estan tirando la tierra." I stopped the car abruptly, put it in park, turned and gave her a hug that was met with more sardonic remarks. Our conversation morphed into what some might consider a morbid conversation. The question of our final wishes and our remains needed a platform and deserved the dignity of time for discussion. Again, I included jokes to lighten the mood, part of my duties; our moments had to be both sober and insane.

So, I stated to her that the little creatures that nibble away at our remains eat at our tongues first and foremost. She squirmed in her seat as an unconvinced eye examined my statement. The question, "Why?" was forthcoming. I looked into her inquisitive gaze, and with a straight face, expanded my nonsense. "So, they don't hear your screams when they're eating out your booty." She let fly a knuckle sandwich that did some damage; she could still pack a wallop. Further, I declared that when the time came I was going the cremation route. She laughed and offered maybe she would do the same. Apparently, as she was approaching her nineties, thinking about her nalgas getting molested, or any such sexual activities, was less appealing to discuss than even the topic of death and burial. I joked it would be slim pickings from us, since neither of us had much of a butt cushion to begin with. The volume of our laughter bellowed as we resumed along the rickety road.

The trips to the cold marble at St. Michael's Cemetery always left me feeling better than when I arrived. Those moments of recollection which clung as permanent reminders that love was always a big part of my growing process. But as was to be expected, La Vieja was hungry so I pressed the fast forward button on my reminiscing and headed to La Conga for some rice, beans, and picadillo. At the end of that long day I made my way up the steps which segregated Foforito and me.

The following morning a sense of urgency encouraged me to sprint directly to my journal to write before my thoughts evaporated. I straddled the hammock that created the makeshift dayroom portion of my bedroom, officially settled into my swaying time capsule. The subtle sway of the suspended cords crisscrossed with reflections of sunlight throughout the space. Corner houses are light bound; my home was flooded with an abundance of it. A few pillows had found their way to places that welcomed them. The sun's shifting provided different angles of energizing light as I began to flirt with the word on the lineless paper. *Intrusion...* a title suggested by Denise when I had told her I was thinking of writing a memoir in three parts. *Intrusion... was that too harsh?* My tangled thoughts zig-zagged like the sun's rays and the hammock ropes. No question, I loved my mother, but would *Intrusion* appear as a contradiction? It wouldn't be a misprint that I didn't like the person she was becoming, especially since she was now my fulltime roommate. Love has variances. When I researched the word in the thesaurus I found encroachment, invasion, incursion, disturbance, disruption, interruption... *Oh yeah, Intrusion would be appropriate.* The music in the background caused me to travel to yet another poignant moment. I was surveying books, and collectables in this room, where Marvin Gaye's, 'What's Going On?' was playing on the radio and the hammock had strapped me in for the ride. Remembrances of my brother Tony were in this room. I found myself back in time.

———————

On Three Kings Day, January 6, 1994 Tony passed away after a prolonged battle with HIV/AIDS. On January 7th, traveling with Al and Yolanda, my mother arrived from California and stayed with me almost until the end of the year. Three months after Tony's passing, we celebrated his life on his birthday. The April gathering was testimony to the fact that Tony had been a very loving people person all his life. A week before the event we diligently made preparations. Foforito had wanted to clean the ceilings, walls, floors, and everything in between. She would be home alone, with the exception of Miel, my cat and Magui, my trusted confidant, a huge Rottweiler. I told Foforito to do only what she could reach, and I would do the rest. Then I left for work.

When I returned home, I found Foforito with a broken wrist and a gash over her eye; she had fallen from a chair while cleaning. The accident happened shortly after I had left in the morning. Remarkably, despite her wounds and injuries, she had washed two loads of clothing, hung them up, bathed herself, and made dinner. Tough girl.

At the time, I didn't have a car, but Omar, a neighbor, dropped us off at the hospital. In the emergency room they took x-rays, set her wrist in a cast, gave her some stitches, and addressed her bruises. All the while, I loudly explained each procedure to her. I was placed in another room and interrogated about how she attained the damage. At first I was insulted by the line of questioning; it was an affront, and I became defensive. I told the police officer I only raised my voice with her because my mother was almost deaf. Additionally, she obviously hadn't paid attention to my warning not to climb on anything while doing the cleaning.

The officer actually was sympathetic, "Hey, I understand. My Moms lives with me; but I gotta ask." I think he also realized that my behavior had been genuinely concerned when I had brought her in.

Back home, even with the cast on, she prepared a spread for royalty and shared her blessing with all the folks who had come with heartfelt thoughts to celebrate. She was also the last one standing the next morning as she and I washed dishes. Even though, her well-intended antics had put her in harm's way and had me addressing the consequences of her actions... *Very tough girl.*

Recollections cradled my thoughts as I continued to write... One of the more amusing episodes was the guilt-trip adventure Foforito mustered when she learned that I was preparing to venture to Cuba with some friends. A Mama's list of concerns and apprehensions were shared over coffee, "a communist country... You'll be detained..."

Those points became moot once I obtained my ticket. Yet Foforito was not discouraged in her attempts to derail my journey. Now she switched to guilt-tripping me about her own health and well-being. Suddenly she developed a limp, to the point where one leg dragged against the floor leaving the floor scuffed. In addition, the thought of being babysat by Elsa, her youngest sister, and Genevieve, the family nun, completely nauseated her. She stood her ground, and shared murky visions of the perils she would endure if something were to happen to me. They were Oscar-worthy performances. The day before I left she knocked on my door with a last-ditch effort. "I want you to be careful. You needn't worry about me." A meek, needy look highlighted her every word. She was working it, and rather convincingly. When she finished her discourse, I thanked her for her concern and told her that I would take her advice under consideration. "You'll be in good hands, and I'll be back before you realize I'm gone." Her pangs of conscience had fallen on unsympathetic ears; which rendered her unsuccessful in her attempts to keep this ball and chain in place. A sour "Que Dios te bendiga" faded as she left the room in a huff, without the dramatic limp that had accompanied her entrance. I chuckled and announced as she descended down the steps, "I see you're feeling better, no more limp." She dismissed me with a wave of her hand that spoke volumes of disgust.

Rousing me from recollection-land, Miel pounced onto the hammock; his insistent meowing announced his desire to be fed. I knew Magui's clumsy canine paws weren't far behind, and he too would be hungry. Startled from my reverie, I prepared supper for the two coolest pets one could ever have. Years later when each had passed away I never contemplated having pets again. This evening after satisfying their dinner demands, I returned to the hammock. Reminiscing resumed in full bloom.

Hammock memories brought to mind that from the time of my father's death (1982) to the time of my brother Tony's death (1994), Foforito had traveled from coast to coast, full of spunk and very mobile. Prior to one of her eastbound trips, my brother Al forewarned that she was in rare form following her recent cataract operation. At the airport she disembarked wearing the Darth Vader glasses. The body language was telling, and the telling wasn't good. As custom dictated, I asked her for her bendiciónes. Without providing them, she began singing her West Coast Blues. Since I wasn't in the mood for her song, I lowered the volume on my hearing aids and nodded on occasion, keeping up the pretense of respect. As she had done every year, upon arriving at Denise's and my home, Foforito immediately revamped our kitchen. I knew the episode would be challenging; I just wanted to keep the peace. Denise's look, although respectful, registered somewhere between aggravated and tolerant. She offered Foforito a plastic container for her false teeth. My mother never used the container. Furthermore, she knew that it irked Denise when she placed the dentures in the drinking glasses we used daily: hygienic hell. So, the teeth floated like specimens in a glass laboratory jar. Needless to say, this wasn't going well.

One day soon after Foforito's arrival, while I was at work, Magui was chewing on his rawhide bone when, in a swift swoop, his head and the rawhide caught the back part of my mother's knee. The blow not only buckled her but caused a large contusion as well. So, forced to limp, Foforito had become keenly cautious of Magui's whereabouts. I guess by association, the cat had also fallen out of favor and had been sent to the doghouse, if you will. Miel got no more treats as Foforito had given him in the past. After a week of being a drag (literally, her foot and figuratively, her attitude), Foforito saw Magui once again engaged with the rawhide bone. Limping into action Foforito grabbed a ball the cat often played with and offered it to Magui as a fair exchange for the offending rawhide bone.

In retrospect, both the truce gesture and the negotiating posture Foforito assumed turned out to be ill-advised. Remember, I mentioned Magui was a little clumsy? As I heard it told, since I wasn't present, my 'best friend' pawed at the ball but caught my mother's eye because she was too close in her trade-off position. Luckily, I arrived as the drama was playing itself out. In the emergency room they tended to what turned out to be a superficial wound and cleared her to go home. The patch placed over her eye was to be worn until the follow-up visit. Wounded and combative, La Vieja re-entered the house of doom, limping and wearing a patch like an ornery pirate. Over the next few weeks, the friction in the house subtly escalated, as dagger-sharp remarks found their way to intended targets.

Another day had been blissfully beautiful until I turned the key into total upheaval. Everything was ransacked; dresser drawers, closets; disheveled. Foforito was fit to be tied. I tried calming her to find out what was going on. "My teeth," she screamed, "they're gone!" We searched the entire house; nothing. I went to the backyard to see if Magui had dug a hole, I looked through the garbage; nothing. It remained a mystery for a long time. In the interim, Foforito limping and wearing a patch was now without her choppers.

Hopefully, reader, you will excuse me for the following: Foforito had become an outright bitch. Magui was atop her shit list. Poor Magui got blamed for everything from chopper theft to passing gas. Denise, Miel, and I shared second place, depending on who was in closest proximity.

The dust hadn't settled from the false teeth mystery, when one day I arrived home to find her packing. "What's going on here?" She looked at me with reddened eyes and a deflated posture and told me, "Get me a ticket, I don't care what it costs." As it turned out, she had opened the drawer that housed her pure white sanitized bloomers. The ones she would roll up like Cuban cigars and place meticulously to the right of the top drawer. Miel evidently had had his fill with her and pissed on all her panties.

The following morning, I took my mother to the airport and placed her on a flight to California. I forewarned my brother of what was in store. Foforito was limping, had a patched eye, was adjusting to her second set of choppers and was wearing stained underwear. Al called to let me know she had arrived, complaining and throwing dirt on the entire clan back East. I went shopping that day and got a beautiful T-bone steak for Magui and some tuna fish for Miel. These were just rewards for a job well done, albeit unsolicited.

Intrusion? Absolutely.
Over and done? Absolutely not!

Here is the footnote, respectfully submitted to anyone inquisitive about what happened to my mother's false teeth. Years after my mother passed away Denise confessed to me that after days of not knowing what to do about hygiene hell in the drinking glasses, she had taken the teeth and disposed of them. Upon reflection, I can't say that I blamed her; unbeknownst to me at the time, she had been subjected to my mother's venom. Later, In the odd communication dance that happens among family members, I exonerated Denise for her act of frustration and self-defense; I also asked her forgiveness for my being oblivious. Following a respectable period, Denise and Foforito had been able to break bread, as moving forward my mother had started to mellow; and Denise forgave.

Foforito, (back from California and now throwing dirt on the Western clan... but you already know that) also had a rash. She constantly scratched both her legs and her left arm. Her right arm, the only limb free of the irritated, scaly skin was menacing the other three with the ripping-style scratching. Patrolling the issue was no easy task; lotions worked in spurts. She was like a junkie feeding a habit. The relief after a good scratch was addicted to the next itch until infection set in. If my mother had been provided a formal education, she could have been a lawyer. In defense of her scratching, she presented the argument that while watching the games I would scratch my balls. I must admit she was right. *But I didn't draw blood,* I thought to myself. Staying the course as her caretaker, I manicured her nails, so they were no longer able to assist the rude destruction of flesh. Calamine lotion, in combination with other ointments and antibiotic creams, brought hope. She began kicking the urge to scratch; the wounds showed signs of healing. Every day I applied and massaged those limbs so telling of her history.

And so, I wrote. I went from pounding on the computer keys, abusing them until they were grey and ashy, to extended periods of neglect. In part, my composing pen had been arrested for being over-analytical. Reluctantly, I was feeling insecure about my limitations of grammar and proper English. The classroom had never been a place that made me feel at ease. I decided that to educate myself would be too huge a hurdle given the circumstances and the obvious duties at hand. Being Foforito's son, I had inherited the perfectionist gene; it was an itch. I was tweaking every sentence until I abandoned the project.

Then the itch became a rash: the more I scratched, the worse it festered. Unattended wounds infect our well-being on so many levels. One's hands, when read properly, highlight in detail the travels and the travesties that accompanied the crossing.

The hankering to write was insistent. I started tickling the keyboard. It felt romantic, fresh; the reunion was exhilarating. I guess editors will scratch their heads upon undertaking this story. Hopefully, with their trained eyes, they can make sense of the misplaced commas, multiple languages, and so-ons of my journey. Period.

Taking care of my mother full-time taught me things. Immediately I realized Foforito and I needed help... and I needed to get away for a few days to regroup. I called my "joint custody" partner, Al, to activate our custodial arrangements. When the deal had been done that our mother would no longer be living in California with Al and family, Al had agreed to head east from time to time and stay at my home to help me with our mother. I pushed the envelope. "Bro, I need to catch my breath. Can you handle Foforito on your own for a few days?" At the time both my brother and I were separated from our wives. Al understood my situation and encouraged me to take some time for myself.

Having cleared the hurdle of ascertaining Medicaid services I was able to call an agency for a home attendant. The assignment would be to assist Foforito with grooming, some meals, a little exercise and a little conversation, preferably in Spanish. The agency would arrange to send someone the following Monday, Now for my getaway. I called the airlines and booked a flight to Puerto Rico; I would leave two days after my brother arrived in New Jersey. In those two days, according to plan Al and I developed a rhythm with Foforito, which included preparing her for the lady who was coming. Foforito was surprisingly receptive to the idea of having a female attendant. On Monday Foforito, Al and my pets would be in New Jersey; I would be in Puerto Rico.

Attendant One reported to work just before noon on Monday. She mumbled a vague excuse for being three hours late for her first day on the job. When Al answered the door to let her in, he had already helped Foforito to bathe, groom, dress and have her breakfast. He was beginning to prepare lunch. These tasks were on the agency accountability sheet which Al or I would sign at the end of the work week. For the rest of the first day, and the next couple of days Attendant One assumed a sit and watch posture. Al called me each day to report that the woman either arrived late or asked to leave early and was consistently 'hands off' with our mother. Foforito, was very annoyed, especially when the woman tried to 'make nice' with condescending pats on my mother's back. My brother forewarned me "You should see La Vieja cut this woman her best, "Don't touch me!" look. It's almost funny. I don't think this lady is gonna work out for you, Lil' Brother, 'cause she's not working out for Mom."

Back home, I joined Al to reset our "Foforito Care" schedule despite the fact that Attendant One arrived late and then one day not at all. Foforito expressed her displeasure every step of the way. I was down a co-pilot as

Al was on his way back to California. On what would be Attendant One's last day, I announced that I needed to run some errands and would return shortly. When I got to the car I realized I'd forgotten the package I wanted to mail and returned to the house. My mother was on the first floor, alone at the dining table where I had left the two women sitting. My mind went straight to worst case scenario. *What's going on? Where is the woman? Did Foforito lock her in the pantry?* I could see the headlines: *Health Care Attendant locked in a closet by disgruntled elder! Calm down*, I told myself.

"Vieja, where is the home attendant?" Foforito put two fingers of her left hand over her lips in a gesture of secrecy. She used the pointer finger of her right hand to point above her head towards the ceiling. Following Foforito's silent directions, I went up the stairs where I discovered the missing home attendant in the living room. She was relaxing in the recliner, watching a Spanish soap opera on the television. In one hand she had a bottle of water, in the other hand she was holding the television remote control. Well, you know... "Good-bye, Miss Soap Opera." "Hello, Health Care Agency, can you please send me...?" This process was repeated on four occasions over the next few months.

I hoped maybe Attendant Five might be the one. She was younger than the previous attendants and didn't speak Spanish, which limited conversation with my mom. Regardless, I tried to think positively that she would accomplish the caretaking. While I took care of Foforito's needs, Attendant Five sat next to my mother... doing her homework. Five's focus was more on her school assignment and less on making sure La Vieja didn't need something, or worse fall off the chair. One day, two days. On the third day Attendant Five's boyfriend rang my doorbell an hour before the end of the workday.

Rudely, the young man announced that he was there to pick up his girlfriend and demanded that she come with him, immediately. When I asked if there was an emergency, he impatiently, informed me that he didn't intend to leave and come back in an hour. He was there to take his girlfriend with him, "Now!"

During my sixth call to the agency, my complete frustration lead me to swear that this would be my final attempt to use their services to provide an adequate home care attendant. Since I had the option to choose another agency, I decided to challenge the present one. I regurgitated my frustrations. We had already suffered through attendants who were perpetually tardy and attendants who were disengaged. One girl spent her tour doing her homework; another asked if I could make her some coffee, as opposed to (by the job definition) her preparing coffee and lunch for my mother. Of course, the kicker was the one on my recliner watching television as my mother sat unattended in another part of the house. Clearly, it had been difficult to trust strangers with my elder and in my home.

The manager was very affable; she arrived with a replacement and assured me that this would be a good fit. Aida, a stout and stern, Peruvian woman was a convincing candidate.

The sixty-six years old, devout Catholic, had a no-nonsense demeanor, and a smile you could tie into a knot on the top of her head. It also helped that the first three letters of her name spelled "aid". Presenting my concerns, I made her aware of my mother's maladies. As the conference came to an end Aida revealed to me that she would be retiring the following year but would tend to my mother's needs until that day arrived. She did.

Foforito gave Aida the head-to-toe inspection and allowed her entry into her domain. At first, it seemed like a match made in heaven. Aida was on time, performed all her duties, and engaged my mother in dialogue and dominoes. The Health Care allotment only provided for twenty-eight hours of service; I still needed additional aid. Previously, out-of-pocket, I had enlisted part-time services from Miriam and also hired Lourdes to come in for a few hours on Saturdays. Anticipating Aida's retirement, I negotiated with the agency to hire Miriam with full-time hours. This would mean less out-of-pocket from my not so full pockets. Later, when Aida retired, Miriam became my mother's full-time home attendant; the replacement was a smooth one.

These women's pampering of my mother provided me moments to gather myself and become somewhat more social and productive. Hallelujah! Finally, I had a support system in place. That elevated my spirit. I must admit it was a profound period that resurrected my views towards our humanity. Knowing that my mother was in secure hands provided me a new lease on life; I had a bounce in my stride.

Over time Aida became as family. This evolution happened because she performed her job seriously which lifted a little weight off my shoulders and allowed me to maneuver more efficiently with my new responsibilities. Then one day I gave Aida a peck on the cheek when she arrived; after all, we had become a team and things were going smoothly. Dark green jealousy reared its ugly head; Foforito was filled with a boatload of insecurity. She became condescending and confrontational. If Aida was washing dishes, Foforito wanted to do them; the wedge was in. Protecting her interests at any cost, Foforito viewed anyone who showed me kindness as a threat to her security. Aida offered her resignation if that would make my mother more comfortable. I needed to salvage this relationship until her retirement; good help was in short supply. Starting over would be no picnic.

Aida was hands on and would think on her feet. For instance, when Foforito had a scheduled visit with her primary care doctor, I felt comfortable leaving her at the clinic entrance in Aida's care. Without having to worry about Foforito's safety while I parked the car, I was enabled to search for and find a spot nearby and quickly. When I returned to the clinic entrance Aida had already taken Foforito inside. These medical-care places could kill you, figuratively, or make you sick, literally. With a deep breath, I made a note to take better care of myself in the present, to avoid becoming a senior needing to navigate the medical-care maze in the future.

The waiting room was crammed with folks suffering from ailments that, in all likelihood, would not be addressed in that office. For all practical purposes, this was a pill-dispensing facility. Thinking back, I had found it hilarious that television commercials were laced with miracle drugs that in time would make the liver quiver. During prime-time programming, drugs are pitched; then, during late-night programming lawyers advertised they would defend those wanting to sue the drug companies for side effects suffered caused by the drugs pitched earlier in the day. Around the room were sullen faces on those seeking answers to their afflictions; chatting about their maladies. Some were full of hope, some were just disillusioned. Being cynical allowed me a clear view of the con job. Each of three tiny cubicles in the rear housed a patient waiting for the doctor's attention. With my guidance, Foforito found her way to one of the booths and got propped onto the examining table. Her perfumed Maja soap filled the enclosure with elegance. A spotless white blouse adorned by her personalized, creative touch sat on brittle shoulders, creating a dainty view of the huggable curmudgeon. Slowly and gently, she removed her blouse, exposing one of the tee shirts which Al had sent her by the dozens. She wore them religiously and washed them whiter than white. Embedded in her memory must have been the beatings she received in her youth for not having washed clean enough, even as she abused the washboard in trying.

Foforito shivered from the chill in the room. The tacky accordion door assured her privacy as we awaited the roaming doctor. Old rugs housed vintage dust in this dingy and unkempt place. Against the walls behind the reception area were metal shelves littered with file folders and papers. To amuse myself by staring at the antiquated filing system every time I saw it. On the shelves were thousands of folders. The folders contained the files that logged patients' wellness, although more often defined illnesses and eventual demise. Those files were probably millions of pages. I couldn't imagine relocating and filing that clutter of questionable information in order to paint the walls. I started thinking, *I wonder if those ancient, pre-digital records would work as permanent wallpaper? No, my friend, private medical records on public display, as wallpaper? Get serious, you know that's illegal. Are you kidding?*

At the time, holistic awareness and alternative medicine weren't covered under social services, so we were forced to comply with the 'use it or lose it' benefits of the what i called the Seven-Minute Plan. Typically, the doctor entered the cubicle, checked blood pressure, pulse, reflexes. Then with a pat on the shoulder, said, "You'll be fine," and out. Seven minutes. Her general practitioner had been popping in and out of each tiny room in a huff; after all, time is money. On cue, he popped into the cubicle Foforito was in and checked her blood pressure; 120 over 80, perfect. Her pulse was spot on; reflexes also flawless. It was a utopian prognosis, which when I translated she clenched both her fists claiming victory, and then gave him a double high five. He asked how her mental state had been lately. My response was concise and to the point, "She's getting very confrontational, forgetful, and repetitious." He proposed medication for her aggressive behavior. "Save the ink; I don't need her to become more unstable on her already-rickety legs. Nope, no anti-cranky drugs, I'll deal with her cranky ways." He shrugged his shoulders, then turned to her and told her, "You're going to be around for another twenty years." It was music to her ears.

I reviewed his statement which sent a chill down my spine. *Twenty years, shit, I'll be eighty.* The thought depressed me. Good news could be staggering, even heart-wrenching. I mockingly grabbed my heart and fell to one knee clutching his arm. He didn't get the humor, but I could not have cared less. Foforito was hungry. In a hurried tone, doc asked, as if he didn't have time for her response, "What are you having?" I responded in like cadence, dripping with wit and sarcasm, "Some chicken soup, and an apple."

Such recollections were a springboard for the journey before me. The humorous twists made the road less bumpy.

JOURNEY

THE SOUNDS WHICH SILENCE MADE, once so comforting, were now a cruel reminder of my personal negligence. When I removed my hearing aids, the clave beat of waves on the shore evaporated instantly. Such was life when I couldn't backtrack on self-imposed abuses. A dive into welcoming waters shattered my dream. I awakened in my bed, not wanting to drown in my own sweat, clutching the poor pillow like a lifesaver. Stretching, I reminded myself of the Tin Man, in The Wizard of Oz. Even prior to inserting my hearing aids, I could almost hear his legendary clanking in my mind. With my "Better to hear you with, my dear" devices in place, I was enabled to confront Foforito's morning gripes. As usual, in her designated cubbyhole by the window, she was mumbling to no one, or anyone who would listen.

Prying past the window cove full of plants, rays of sunlight nestled around Foforito's locks giving her an angelic look. I had come to appreciate that look and hoped wasn't false advertising. The only thing missing were the wings I'm sure she'd earned by then. She had made mention on numerous occasions that a trip to Puerto Rico was an item on her bucket list.

"Come sit here," she patted the neighboring chair. Usually that meant she had concerns and wanted to convey them as part of a dream she'd had. Often my dad got injected into this equation since his logic always had been the voice of reason. "M'ijo, my boat is taking in too much water." Her statement was telling in that she was aware of her medical and mental situation; her statement was urgent. Her words resonated in my mind like a scratched-up LP record. In the past, traveling with my mother was mostly friction-free. Given her present state (the screws upstairs were a little loose—and some were stripped altogether), I anticipated that preparing for and accomplishing this trip would be a monumental task. Nonetheless, I couldn't shake her statement or its connotations. It was one of many that are so profound in their simplicity. "My boat is taking in too much water." How appropriate.

I began nurturing the thought of embarking on her request. The journey was sprouting legs. Under normal circumstances she became discombobulated in preparation for travel. It would be a little unnerving with no female companion to assist with delicate matters. Just mi vieja and me for a month or so; I took a deep breath.

Perhaps I could talk myself out of doing it; although I understood not being able to live with myself if her plea went unanswered. This phase of my life with my mother— one of acceptance—reshaped my views as I embraced the moments shared from that day forward.

Foforito's past was muddled with dementia's demons lurking at every turn. She recalled her youth, an abusive past that had scarred her, both physically and emotionally, to date. Rehashing those invasive moments always conjured unresolved issues. I was optimistic the trip could help her to resolve some of them. At the time she was having a problem remembering what she just had for breakfast, but the awful reminders of disallowed youth stuck to her external hard drive ready to download at a moment's notice. Her present, saturated with liabilities, left her frustrated, disorientated and frequently incoherent. The last, concerned me the most. Her tomorrows, sketchy at best and riddled with mounting afflictions both real and imagined, had Foforito in a constant tiff with herself. So, she carried on, uneasy, unsteady and very confrontational. The weeks leading up to our departure were trying and tested my patience to its limit. The pilgrimage had me emotionally staggered, and we had not even set sail.

My battered expression told the story. It turned out that none of the Medicaid homemakers, nor out-of-pocket babysitters were going to be part of the crossing. That thought left me rattled. I had figured offering the tropical breezes, as opposed to the howling winds, would be a welcomed trade-off, not only for me, but for anyone accompanying us on our journey. My own bones chattered at the acute thought of the damage winter added to my well-being. Whenever I mistakenly believed that I'd retired my trade, my barking bones reminded me that it was my trade that had retired me. Since no one accepted my barter plan, it would be just Foforito and me escaping from the northeast winter winds. With two weeks left to take-off, La Vieja was packing and unpacking daily. From dawn to dusk... packing, unpacking, packing, unpack... Well, you get the picture.

Although her breathing was labored, she defiantly refused when I had offered to lend a hand. It was heart-wrenching to watch her painstaking search. Foforito's bras were missing, again. With an iron grip, she stubbornly clung to doing for herself. In the next frenzied moments, she complained, blamed, fussed, cursed, kicked, pulled her hair. She delicately bit herself in a gesture of total frustration. When all else failed, her teary, guilt-trip game began. Bras, eyeglasses, and so on... GONE, if only in her mind... To better navigate my mother's universe, without interfering with her limited independence, I took to studying the scavenging patterns of squirrels in my backyard. Apparently, using similar hiding habits, Foforito commandeered half of my three-tiered house for misplacing her prized possessions. My mother sentimentally treasured her old bras. Those vintage garments had housed the welcoming breasts she had surrendered to my father. She believed not having her lingerie was a sacrilege, a crime. Then, I got an idea! I told Foforito I'd contact a detective to conduct a proper investigation for The Case of Missing Stuff. It worked! That imaginary detective became my hero.

Just as my mama zippered the suitcase, I snatched it and took it to the upper floor, where too many steps served as a buffer. The following day she was still frantic. I settled her in her breakfast perch and told her that new airport guidelines required luggage to be delivered prior to departure. So, in compliance, ours was already there. Hopefully, her God would forgive me for lying to my own mother. She took the bait but looked at me suspiciously out the corner of her eye. I had to make arrangements for leaving my car here, and the rental there. I had to pay bills, get a plant sitter; the to-do list was extensive.

Identification documents for travel, medication, which she always managed not to take. I even arranged to mail some toiletries and other necessities ahead of time. I even packed a hand-held recorder so I wouldn't have to rely on my memory of the conversations that would happen during the next month. Getting ready for that trip was a trip.

Careful preparations for the adventure were rewarded. I convinced myself all would fall into place, and the universe agreed. Yogui arrived at the designated time to drive us to the airport. Foforito was seat belted in, and luggage containing clothing and supplies for thirty days was placed in the rear of the car. The pre-dawn airport appeared abandoned; an eerie feeling came over me. Tumbleweed was the missing ingredient on that set. The unfounded, heightened state of alertness started to dissipate as we cleared TSA without incident. Traveling with elders had its benefits and Foforito can be adorable when need be. With three hours to kill before takeoff we settled in and chatted until our jaws ached.

Boarding the plane was a breeze, and we had great seats—close to bathroom, next to the exit. A window seat provided my mother a pageant view of the gathering clouds. As they mushroomed, the visual stimulation worked wonders to captivate her imagination. The gift to me was a moment to exhale and converse with a fellow construction worker sandwiched between Foforito and me. When I divided up the food provisions I had prepared and brought onboard, there were enough to include the electrician, whose name I never found out.

With bellies full, my companions decided to nap; giving me some alone time for a few hands of solitaire.

Touchdown, like liftoff, was smooth. Our luggage found its way onto the baggage carousel like Siamese twins. All transitions went according to plan, including the car rental and the weather. With the preliminary obstacles out of the way, we headed to Bebo's, a famous food stand in Carolina, for some rotisserie chicken and yuca. As was our custom, my mama and I started inhaling oil-laden foods from the quiosco that populated the countryside. Afterwards we compared greasy lips as laughter filled the air-conditioned car. We plowed forward, hunger-free and content.

Sleeping accommodations for the month we would be in Puerto Rico were provided by the generosity of family members. Primarily, we stayed in the home of Doña Lydia, my mother-in-law, who lives in Carolina. On a couple of overnight side trips, we stayed with family in Naranjito and Comerio. Foforito and I knew our way around the island and would not have to inconvenience our hosts for escort services. Upon arriving at Doña Lydia's, our first stop after lunch, we dropped our bags, visited briefly and prepared to head out for some rations.

Pueblo supermarket had all our needs on its shelves in abundance. We become separated, and the first Foforito search was underway. Finally, a sighting! She is there by the dessert section at the bakery stand. I should have known, as even her false teeth had a sweet tooth, which made me wonder if they had been made out of a fructose-craving material. Foforito had had a pastry Jones for as long as I could recall. If one wanted to coax or win her over, bribery with pastries did the trick. Whenever she would devour a dessert an orgasmic moan punctuated the moment like an operatic crescendo. My mother had reached a cuddly, affectionate stage of communication, so I surrendered to her fetishes, as long as she behaved. But I'll tell you, it wasn't easy raising a parent, especially a stubborn one with mule-kick-to-the-gut attributes. Heading back to the car, she placed her hand around my waist. Instinctively I dropped my arm down on her shoulder as she mumbled awkwardly, "Gracias, m'ijo." In turn, I sprouted emotions that had been misplaced, ignored, and/or buried out of convenience. A salty liquid gathered on my eyeglasses as I walked into the uncertainties this journey would no doubt provide.

Back at our home away from home, we settled in and began organizing our personal belongings. Foforito popped out of her designated room dressed to impress and informed me that a lucky itch she was having in her hands was a sign of good fortune. She wanted to visit a casino to cure what she labeled..., "a craving." I thought, *addiction was a more appropriate term.* After splashing some cold water on my face, I rummaged through my suitcase for my *Driving Miss Daisy* chauffeur cap. Following the splash, a passing look revealed my worn-out appearance, wincing under the responsibility of unwanted leadership. I freshened up a bit more and changed from my travel clothing into a tee shirt and jeans. La Vieja criticized my casual outfit, noting that my veneer wasn't polished to her liking. To accommodate, I changed clothes, *again.* I put on a shirt she had sewn for me, one of many that I safeguarded in zippered plastic covers. While choosing a shirt. I had to admit she had no rivals when it came to showing off her skills in her trade.

Once we reached the casino in Isla Verde, so conveniently close to our present abode, I pandered to La Vieja's fickle obsession. I opened the door for Her Majesty and proceeded to settle her at the machine she desired. Then I sought someone to watch over her needs—soft drinks, perks, anything that would heighten this regal woman's ego.

The hostess/cocktail waitress, dressed in a provocative uniform, complimented me on the shirt I was wearing. Foforito gave me the "I told you so" look and gave herself credit for its origin. "I make his underwears, too." She even offered the scantily clad young lady her own jacket commenting, "You must be cold wearing next to nothing."

My mother had a knack for being brutally blunt. As quickly as the waitress blushed, I apologized for Foforito's comment. Professionally, our hostess admitted it was cold in the casino and thanked my mother for what graciously was handled as a goodwill gesture. With that, three twenty-dollar bills were fed into the one-armed bandits, and La Vieja was in her zone. She got spanked, as they say, but the thrill of lights, sounds and excitement swirling around her had been rejuvenating. I, on the other hand, was drained from the duty-saturated marathon I had been running. After a couple of hours, she finally called out to me that she had had her fill; that was music to my ears. Back in Doña Lydia's quiet neighborhood the disturbance caused by the Mister Softee ice cream truck impersonator and an occasional bull-horned preacher stirred up the dogs. I never saw any of them but despised all the noise. Despite the barking, we packed it in for the night. It had been an incredibly long day.

The following day called for creative compromise to be sure; I needed to feed my addiction as a sun worshiper. Once we devoured a ham-and-egg-and-fries heart attack special, we mounted the rented wheels and headed on Ruta 3 to Luquillo Beach. The scenery along the way filled her with memory and she recited folks' names, as well as feelings that came to mind. I'd taken note that as my mother's hearing loss had progressed she compensated by nonstop verbiage. In doing so, it seemed to allow her to not feel like she was in a vacuum, an ambience I was all too familiar with. We parked and started our beach-bound trek like two carefree happy campers. I settled her things under a shady palm tree and placed her next to them in a beach lounge chair. The shore was silent, practically vacant, and void of children's laughter. Calm waters, absent of waves, seduced me to wade into that Caribbean heaven.

A recent spiritual reading had suggested that I do seven dips backwards and scrub with seaweed. The first thrust imitated the sound of hot frying pans submerged into cold water. I complied with the spiritual prescription as I frolicked freely in the salty, tasty, sea. In the medicinal aqua blue, I went from being weighted down like a beast of burden, to feeling weightless without a concern or worry. *The ocean can be such a healer: the water, the salt, the ambience.* That invigorating dip into the sea was uplifting and long overdue. When I exited and walked back to the towel, the warmth from the sand migrated north through me from feet to crown; it was delightfully surreal. I felt rewarded, blessed, and validated. The reassuring bounce in my walk and the clear view of the horizon further hinted of healing. Fragmented feelings were coming together towards making me feel whole again. I patted myself dry, exhaled and began scribbling in my note pad.

When I looked over my shoulder for Foforito, she was nowhere to be seen. The beach chair had been abandoned. Prayer books, and knitting threads sat unattended, along with her wallet and I.D. *SHIT! Where could she be?* A heart-pounding anxiety took hold as my eyes scoured the landscape of erect palm trees and of tourists ascending onto the beach. *Get a grip! Get a grip!* My accelerated heartbeat gave way to cautious panic. I gathered my belongings and tried to reason her whereabouts. I understood in part a parent's nightmare upon losing sight of a child—the horror! Dark thoughts entered my mind. My knees buckled. I pictured myself stapling posters worded: 'Lost and Vulnerable—ninety-one-year-old woman—wild Einstein hairdo—bata and slippers.' As in the casino and the supermarket, disappearing was not a first for her. The cynical side of me said, *Could this be my escape clause? Good riddance.* I chuckled nervously at the thought. Instinctively I headed to the bathroom facilities. Foforito couldn't be too far off, she takes turtle steps—unless she's bathroom bound. As I approached the ladies' room I found myself yelling, "Ma!" At the entrance, I almost ran her over. I patted myself on the back for my brilliant deduction; by all accounts, from panic to a Sherlock Holmes in moments.

La Vieja had a desperate expression painted onto her now pink wrinkled cheeks. She looked up at me, relieved and frustrated. Holding her pants halfway down her frail limbs, imitated the street thugs' showing of bloomers. The other hand waved over her unkempt hair as if possessed by some ungodly spirit. "There's no toilet paper in these filthy bathrooms. I have to take a shit." I retrieved some paper from the men's room, equally as grimy as its counterpart. Obviously bothered by her actions, I was nonetheless impressed by her ability to recognize her surroundings and independently tend to her needs. I exhaled and let her know in one breath, that she should make me aware of her whereabouts. And so, reunited, I had that *'Want to squeeze you, then pull your ear'* moment. Welcome to parenting.

Foforito knew exactly which buttons to press to send me over the edge. That morning prior to leaving for the beach, as usual, she couldn't find her bra. "I put my bra here. There's a demon in this house," she proclaimed. Obviously, the previous night's packing and repacking had relocated those items she just could not live without. She turned to me and gave me the accusing eye. Normally, that 'It's just you and me' look created a knee-jerk reaction; but I was cool. After a twenty-minute bra hunt, I felt my energy being sapped. Timeout. She anchored herself to the sofa and refused to budge. I countered with, "I'm going to the beach with or without you." I guess she realized it would be a lonesome day on the couch; the bra fell from the heavens. Without skipping a beat, she gathered her keep-busy belongings, jumped into her bata and found her way to the car. Once in the car everything was fine, she was in her groove. I felt as if I just finished wrestling alligators. My immediate method for maintaining sanity was reining in my emotions to better navigate past all the uncertainties before me.

Frustration and irritation at her lack of ability to focus and reason invited delusional behavior. Foforito grappled with her transitional phase. Lack of acceptance, one of her strong suits, further complicated her confused state. Contemplative looks of self-doubt revealed that she understood her short-term memory loss. She'd catch herself at times. Her long-term memory, which had always been her strong quality, also started to show some cracks. She tended to forget about her siblings who had passed away; then relived appropriate emotions whenever the roll call was recited. The prayer books were brought forth as she began to exercise her unquestioned and steadfast devotion. Worn, Scotch-taped passages were her constant companions. The Man Upstairs must be very busy, or hard of hearing—*no disrespect intended*—but I was beginning to think the Brother was out to lunch or worse yet, never really home to begin with. Questioning religion, false prophets, and Biblical texts, I petitioned to no one in particular; my faith was *we'll see* at best. I believed you came from a hole, eventually landed in one, and in between everything wholly was force-fed, like terrorist propaganda. Personally, I'm stove bound, *just burn up my remains and scatter me.* That said, I still lit candles and prayed, just in case. *One never knows*—a belief I inherited from my grandmother, Eugenia.

La vieja was probably oblivious to my thoughts. I recalled another tender moment when we had been driving on the back roads in Piñones. I had passed my hand along her thinning locks and told her I loved her. In a steady cadence, she responded, "I love you, too." The raw emotions that gathered at my throat shook me to the core. I tended to warehouse feelings, then when I dusted them off and reviewed the importance of their existence, and their relevance in my evolving life, thus became concurrently overwhelmed and relieved. I couldn't help remembering the macho-man advice my brothers and I received as kids, which sounded odd even back then when we first heard it. "You're a man, and men don't cry." *What a bucket of shit!* Those foolish beliefs regarding sensitivity muddled our outlooks and left unresolved issues. The luxury of exorcising those intimate sentiments was refreshing and liberating as my moms and I rolled to our next destination.

The good news was, my mama knew how to entertain herself. She was putting the finishing touches on a flower-printed tapestry she had filled in with crayon-colored threads. Even at this late stage, her attention to detail was commendable. She volleyed between needlepoint and rosary beads as the ocean breezes serenaded her naps. I allowed myself a moment of total relaxation. Emitting those sentiments led me to recognize just how wound up I had been in that tormented period. Letting it go provided me a moment to recharge and arrange the plans necessary to make our trip both meaningful and memorable. Once I had my fill of sun, sand and warm water I suggested we fetch some tacos with crabmeat, and cold coconut water. She put her stamp of approval on my suggestion, claiming that she was starving. Since I was the one in charge, I was responsible to quiet those hunger pains. For as long as I can recall my mother had heaped blame on others for just about anything. I guess doing so was to deflect attention from her own shortcomings and avoid being in the spot-light or in any controversy. It made sense that those were defense mechanisms she had developed to survive as the second oldest sibling, first female, and most abused of the clan. We filled ourselves beyond self-satisfaction como dos sapos de latrina as our mutual smiles acknowledged the moment.

Arm in arm, we waddled to the car and made our way to the supermarket for basic breakfast goods. Oatmeal, farina, coffee, milk, bread, eggs and some sweets to supplement the roadside fetishes quickly filled the shopping cart. Satisfied with the choices, I started toward the check-out counter; Foforito was no longer with me! She had disappeared. In the distance I saw a little old lady, with silver hair, on wobbly legs, in gray pants (void of a rump). She was eyeballing some pastries. I remembered as a child being harnessed due to my inquisitive nature. The thought of putting her on a leash fleetingly crossed my mind and caused me to shake my head and chuckle. The anxiety, although temporary, put me on high alert.

Back at our temporary digs, the compulsive behavior of arranging and rearranging took hold once again, driving her into a frenzy, once again. Misplaced garments signaled ensuing chaos. It was painful to watch. Imagining I might be headed to a similar fate, pained me more. I had begun developing methods to cope with those episodes of despair. So far on the trip they'd proven unsuccessful. La Vieja clung to her possessions with a lockdown hold. I began to glance over her scattered wardrobe, all handmade; it filled me with pride to examine the intricate designs and impeccable detail. As a craftsman, I was in total awe and admiration of her unparalleled skills and level of professionalism. She had engrained those traits in me; maybe "force-fed" would be a better way of explaining my own anal and perfectionist inheritance. An assortment of blouses on the bed formed a jigsaw puzzle soon to be organized and then dumped, in repeat mode, back into the valise. My compliments shifted her attention, but only momentarily, as getting a handle on what was floating inside her mind was a fruitless, painful endeavor. Generally, I volleyed between sympathy and frustration and made note to overdose myself on gingko biloba before entering that stage of my life in the future. Herbs would also assist with my duty of thinking for two people in the present.

A few days after we arrived in Carolina and had settled in we decided to take an expedition to Naranjito and Comerio, home to the roots that unearthed my mother. My mood meter swung erratically. I was cautiously confident that the bending road would lead to uncover revelations to unanswered questions as I tried to better understand this complex, and now discombobulated, woman. What was real and what was imagined was a flip of the coin. Things could go from concrete to quicksand in a heartbeat. While her moods swayed in a lethargic breeze, a stagnant humidity stifled my already limited outlook. Driving behind a dinosaur of a truck emitting clouds of exhaust fumes nauseated me. The cars, zooming recklessly down narrow, twisting roads free of embankments irritated me. Foforito was pointing out sights that were reconnecting her to the time that helped shape the person she presently was. To add to the madness, the recording device I had packed for capturing insightful conversations was nonfunctioning and had abandoned me. I would have to rely on my memory. "You see that cemetery? That's where your grandfather is buried... See that house over there?" My attention was drawn to the white crosses, shrines planted along the road that only raised nightmare thoughts of having my name on one of them.

Finally, we arrived in Naranjito at my Uncle Benny's home, a wonderful spread with a huge wraparound verandah overseeing the landscape below. The land in Naranjito was so lush I remember thinking to myself, *If I spit a piece of Bazooka gum on this soil, a bubblegum tree would grow right here.* Benny, one of fifteen brothers and sisters, welcomed us. As customary, he offered us treats and then invited us for breakfast at his favorite local restaurant. The offer of tripe soup and white rice on the breakfast menu hadn't changed since the inception of this greasy spoon: my kinda place. Over breakfast, Foforito's ability to highlight details of her past was alive and well as she spouted the names of the folks who had shared those moments with her. Gradually, I softened from the tense drive along the mountainside. Grabbing pen and pad from my ever-present backpack, I began scribbling our earlier conversations which were taking on lives of their own. My fried ham and eggs arrived, and it actually took eight napkins to sponge up the oil soup that accompanied the eggs. I lived for these moments: real, raw, unscripted. Admittedly, this was a way of life that clogged the arteries; at the same time, it caused my heart to smile. A f t e r breakfast, with Benny in tow, heading to Eloisa's home in Comerio was another mountain-scape adventure. More white crosses sprouted like flower beds along the way. Caution became the mantra for the remaining moments that escorted us to my auntie's home.

The spirit of struggle was ever present in the person of

Tomásito, Eloisa's forty-one-year-old son, who is mentally challenged. He had an exhaustive list of afflictions that included diabetes, high cholesterol, high blood pressure, and being very aggressive when agitated. He monopolized Elo's calendar, as the daily chores associated with his maladies were without an expiration date or reprieve. Her husband Tomás, a short, plump, jolly figure was only small depending on how one measures folks—head down, or heart up. Tomás was well-educated and an eloquent orator, with independent thought. His socialist ideals, quite frankly, weren't too popular on the island. After being ambushed by a stroke, Tio Tomás sat in a wheelchair, trying to recapture his strength with makeshift weights. Once an enlightening and charismatic personality, he was reduced to struggling with the speech impairment that accompanied the stroke. Regardless, Tio Tomás remained quick-witted and insightful, and refused to relinquish his sense of humor. We shared a hearty hug as our emotions crisscrossed, cheek to cheek. His proficiency in holistic medicine was praiseworthy. He shared the recipes for concoctions and herbal cocktails to combat different ailments. I teasingly crowned him King Shaman of Puerto Rico. A somber mask now veiled his description of the fateful day that derailed his outlook. He shared concerns and the frustration of burdening his lifelong partner. The unwarranted guilt of saddling Elo with further duty saddened him and was evident in his tone. I posed the question, "If the shoe were on the other foot, what then?" He smiled, "Her feet are bigger than mine." And so, he struggled, dependent in large part for basic needs, and with little to no government assistance.

Eloisa appeared aged by responsibility, duty, and her own personal pain. Unable to bend her two bum knees, she navigated by dragging her legs from the hips, as if on stilts. Her heart also needed adjustments, the list of failing body parts was ever-growing. But that list had been placed on a shelf overshadowed by more urgent matters: lunch. She steered the boat in her turbulent sea with a calm that humbled me. Her liabilities dwarfed my personal gripes and difficulties. They didn't make the personal intrusions on my life any less real or painful. Instead, they did allow me to place in context the cross I bore with lucidness and a renewed sense of purpose. Sometimes asking someone, "How you doin'?" can be an inappropriate question. I allowed myself to ask, because I charged myself to take the time to listen. "Aqui, todo bien." She was thankful to be above ground to assist her family as best she could. She had been designated to be in a high-handed arena with no foreseeable outlets, yet in accepting her role, had overcome the calamities placed at her doorstep. "P'alante todo el tiempo," as she swayed her way to tend to others' needs. Her wisdom and spiritual insight dissipated into thin air as she entered Tomásito's lightless room.

Generous to a fault, Eloisa allowed me to invade her downtime. I peppered her with my personal multi-pronged questions about my mother's youth and her recollection of that time period. My mother's umbrage towards her mama remained a point of contention. By way of storytelling, Elo began, "It was a difficult period..."

With a closer look I took note of her wrinkles gouged by a painful history of daily struggles, limited resources and personal loss. Things city folks had taken for granted were non-existent in that rural setting, back then and still. Washing clothing was done in the river on rocks. Food wasn't refrigerated, and religion was force-fed on calloused knees at day's end. Elo's arthritic hands were antsy nested in her lap; a non-challenging smile became faint as she continued to outline the jagged edges of her memory.

By default, the elder females in the clan inherited parenting duties in conjunction with other daily chores associated with farm management. Doña Provi, my grandmother, had become a baby-making machine, without recourse. Foforito had always maintained that, "My mother had them and I raised them." Eloisa confirmed an abusive reality had been heaped on Foforito at such an early age. In silence, her solemn look was telling as she confirmed my mother's comments. In her youth Foforito had been robbed of her free-flowing inquisitive nature and innocence. It was a sad commentary that helped me to grasp the lingering resentments that wreaked havoc over time. Elo went on to conclude that the events of that difficult time left their sibling-scape wounded; especially the child—now old woman—who inherited the bulk of the unjust duty.

Over the years I had learned heavy-handedness was a diplomatic way of labeling the abusive disciplinary methods, unofficially acceptable back in their day. I was told that's just how things were. Foforito had even told me about *inappropriate* activities, *allegedly* committed by a hierarchical figure in the family clan. The topic of abuse could thrust Foforito into the *Hearsay-Blues*. Wrapped in her loss of hearing and memory lapses, I could see my mother had gone somewhere beyond the conversation in the room. She was shaken to the root, wrestling with that unthinkable rumor. *Here we go again!* More than once I had heard Foforito heap praise on the alleged accused, as one of the few sensitive to my mother's daily mistreatment. Her 'hero' had been the bearer of kindness that Foforito's own mother—herself a victim—never provided. With a heightened curiosity for the truth, I had learned to listen between the lines. But, the foul deeds were *never* confirmed to me. I decided to omit discussing the accusations from my line of questioning with Eloisa. In the name of family matters, secrets and answers were taken to the grave as unfinished business. Unsubstantiated or not.

As the day began to end, I become concerned about the ride back to Benny's home. Hazardous enough during daylight, the thought of high beams, drunks, and unfamiliar curves along those winding roads in the dark wasn't appealing to me. *Time to go. We'll be back.* The Puerto Rican goodbyes that one had to undertake as these visits came to conclusion could be draining… and prolonged. I looked at Tomás as he recoiled in his wheelchair, a prisoner of fate. His smile unconvincing, yet cordial, found me kissing him on his forehead. I urged him with my embrace to remain resilient, knowing that being in his place would be a difficult landscape for me to navigate. As always, I reserved my last hug for Eloisa. Her insight, information, and generous spirit had been uplifting for me. We agreed to reconvene within the month to further investigate my inquisitive nature, and those yet-unanswered questions that would accompany it.

In Naranjito, nightfall was when the temperature went

from mountain cool to sudden chill. The day's activities had been a series of checks and balances. I was a bit spent from all the information consumed; but especially curious about what may have been conveniently left unsaid.

Getting reacquainted with Benny reminded me of the days he would socialize with my dad. After a certain age, I was allowed to join them. In those days, boleros hummed in the background; memories danced as the bottle of whiskey evaporated. Foforito, always by the stove, prepared appetizers to sponge up the alcohol. She welcomed company; somehow it provided her a sense of security even at the expense of privacy for us kids in what was a communal setting. Benny enveloped in solitude on this mountaintop was eager to exercise a moment of camaraderie. He sat in the booth he had carved into a niche on the verandah. We began to entertain some clandestine alcohol as Foforito sashayed into our tête-à-tête. As my father's name entered the dialogue, and we sensed his presence also in the booth.

The unrehearsed exchange became a coffee break conversation, in a good way. After all, recalling wisdom, provided without reservation from someone, created gratitude for that someone, regardless of how long they had been absent. In this case, after almost thirty years, Chuito's presence was clearly felt. All we needed were the dominoes. Benny enjoyed company and was a good host. He also appreciated that the steep incline approaching his home created a buffer zone, causing unwanted visitors to be in short supply. Solitude at times allowed reflection, a platform for expression. It could also allow us a chilling view of our vulnerability.

After we had consumed half a bottle of alcohol, Benny stumbled into his quarters. I accompanied my mother, my little butterfly, to her designated cocoon next to my digs, separated only by a bathroom. Foforito, as custom engrained from back in the day, recited the rosary ritual. Since she couldn't hear herself, she shared her recitation with the community at large. Luckily, I had removed my hearing aids and freed my atheist ears from force-fed religion. I lay in the room that was void of fancy amenities. A lamp provided me enough light for me to take a moment to write down the events that had been unfolding.

Those winding roads, fluid as a running brook, were tortuous and unpredictable, yet embracing. In their own way they fostered insight, while cradling and preserving this period in time when I was seeking change. My mother had always been a handful, up to and including this stage of her life. I found myself entangled in a web of indecision, learning the evolution of her journey from all the bends, twists, and turns. The serpentine roads both of Puerto Rico and our lives could be biting or revealing as it uncoiled. Instinctively, I learned that the heart and what it's prepared to offer could take one much further than one's feet. It could also trip one up in the tangle of its emotional strings. As the night started to fade, a glimpse out the window framed a sky full of celestial offerings. Lurking in the lushness, the coquí frogs serenaded me with their lullaby. The thin sheet wrapped around me like a burrito skin partly shielded me from the invasive mosquitoes that had recognized the arrival of new blood. I found myself adrift, one with the sound silence in the countryside brings.

The next morning, a cold shower—the shocking reminder

that I was in the sticks—was nonetheless invigorating. My sugar, Foforito, was having a bad-hair day. The bra thief apparently had entered her space and snatched it. *Now what to do?* I immediately changed the subject, thanking her for repairing a hole in my tee shirt. She had always mended and salvaged my damaged pullovers, which allowed me to maintain my collection. The distraction of gratitude bought me a moment to search for the missing bra. I felt like I had hit the lotto as the misplaced antique had found sanctuary under her pillow.

By default, the greasy spoon was again the breakfast destination. I got into a heated discussion with Foforito over her food selection. Her plate was overloaded with bomb-making material, short fuse and all. Everything she had chosen would make her sick. After all, I was the one who had to deal with the aftermath. Benny looked on, a little bewildered, as we tried to make light of the situation.

As predicted, back at Benny's, Foforito's stomach erupted due to her indiscretions. She had wanted what she wanted, until she had to run to the bowl with a double-ended, one-two punch. Simultaneous diarrhea and vomiting is enough to put the best of us in distress mode; my name got worn out at that needy time. It sounded screechy, overbearing, and even obnoxious depending on her severities. Luckily, Sosa, another aunt down the road, had some manzanilla herbs to calm the stomach. Regardless, diarrhea and vomiting and screeching had already put a damper on the day.

Time has a way of whittling away at our immune system. Foforito's recuperating powers had diminished. A little dehydrated and in need of pampering, the redundant drama of "I'm on my deathbed," was hitting a sour note. I attended to her immediate needs, because this beautiful day could easily have gotten derailed as I was forced to inherit the consequences of her indiscretions.

Resentment tended to cling. I'd realized that her outburst at the casino recently was still festering inside me. My tolerance was taking a beating. My patience needed recharging. As Foforito slipped into siesta mode, I entered my own far-off meditative state. Reviewing and organizing my notes softened my posture and mood enough to take a spontaneous walk. Happily, I was finding objects and natural materials for my art projects, which were creative buffers.

I internalized the cliché that everything happens for a reason. the next morning Foforito awakened looking a little disheveled. With thinning white locks in disarray, and choppers floating in a glass of water nearby, her age was highlighted by the moment. She splashed some water on her face, reached for the Poly-Grip, and combed her shedding mane. Once she was comfortable with her appearance, Foforito proclaimed herself fit for travel. "Let's go," she insisted.

Needless to say, we bypassed the greasy spoon as we headed towards San Juan. But not before Benny and I agreed that the following week he'd take on a babysitting session with his oldest surviving sibling.

La Vieja's latest barrage of tantrums and bipolar-like behavior made me anxious. She could be sweet one minute, moody the next, and then in an instant shoot all the way to volatile. Viewing the panoramic sights on the fringes of the embankments had her teetering on paranoia. After a while, it felt serene as we headed back to the San Juan area. The recorded music on the radio was in sync with the mood and events of the moment. Leaving at close to dawn had us on a road free of other vehicles. An early morning rain had peppered the greenery. Scents from a dense landscape caused a pleasant intoxication. My lungs were in rhythmic glory as they inhaled pure, unadulterated oxygen: holistic heaven. I reached over, gave her shoulder a squeeze and smiled, "Tranquila, Mamita." She had a misty look and fluffy appearance which was welcoming. "Enjoy the moment. You are home," I whispered. The scenic route from town to town was so picturesque that I decided to stay clear of the highways, even if the longer journey cut into sun-worshipping time by the beach. My lungs were grateful. Her attention remained glued to a road, now a time capsule, as was evident by her hypnotized gaze.

Los Van Van, my favorite Cuban musical group, would be performing their farewell concert in Roberto Clemente Stadium later in the month. I would be attending with my friends Pete and his girlfriend Blanca. Foforito spending the night with Benny and Eloisa would leave me duty free. Those thoughts had me perky as Pete and I met briefly to purchase concert tickets.

Days before the concert when I proposed spending some time at the beach, Foforito declined the invitation. She claimed to be a bit under the weather and offered that I go without her as long as I got her some grub to hold her until evening. Music to my ears. In the past I'd talked myself out of selfish, yet good intentions, thus dismissing or trivializing my own time. Conditioning could be brutal. At the juncture of leaving Foforito with Benny and Eloisa for a day, I had, for the moment, allowed myself to feel anxiety-free. Now they would have the opportunity to observe firsthand the trials and tribulations of my reality. Hopefully, their caretaking of my mother would help them to analyze the source and circumstances of my mother's bizarre behavior and off-the-cuff remarks of late.

As I headed to the beach... some thick, gray clouds paraded their way to the seashore. Undeterred, I defiantly forged ahead and parked the car. Attempting to travel light, I had grabbed only a towel, notepad and pen, and almost forgot tanning lotion. My defiance paid off as the clouds fizzled out to sea, clearing the way for blistering beams of unfiltered light.

In times of uncertainty, I summoned my father's virtues, of which he had many. His sense of reason was poetic, witty, and charming. Seeking his guidance in silence, I gazed out at the ocean where a calm had found its way. Pigeons and other birds congregated with obvious liberties and scavenged freely. A handful of tourists and natives walked, jogged, or lazed about, as had I. A walk further found the waves free of visitors. A potent breeze brought some sand in my direction; a new round of water-logged clouds marched towards land.

It was a signal to start packing it in. Whenever I left my Foforito unattended, I shuddered at the scenarios that flooded my brain. Too soon, the guilt trips returned with the intention of shredding my moments of welcomed (and deserved) solitude. I was not in the mood to entertain them. I found myself rushing back to Doña Lydia's home, even though I was doubtful about what lay before me.

My girl was having a heated conversation with someone visible only to her. I sat, eavesdropping on the protracted verbal barrage of unresolved issues with her mother, Doña Provi. I sensed that the verbal attacks she had suffered had been so severe and crippling that her self-esteem was irreparably damaged. I called out her name so as not to unsettle her. Entering the room, I saw she was finishing another rearrangement of her belongings. I purposely shut her suitcase, wrapped my arms around my mother and squeezed until she gave up. Foforito attempted to sneer but was tickled by the affection that apparently had been absent during tender periods of her evolution. She even attempted to corral her joy as if she was unworthy of the tenderness to which she was entitled. I wouldn't have it; I wrestled until she yelled, "Uncle." With my conquering victory secured, I coaxed her to dress so we could go to dinner at one of her favorite eateries, Metropol in Isla Verde, about fifteen minute drive from Doña Lydia's home.

Despite her disheveled state of being, Foforito was tediously aware of her appearance. In her early years, she had been the picture of elegance in rich fabrics. Such grace had been replaced by a set of twins: Poly and Ester. But at that moment, Foforito had a glow. I stepped back to admire her until she blushed and cried out, "Let's go, I'm hungry." She complimented herself for the shirt she had made me.

When we got in the car, she told me I blew it with the dungarees. "Your father, now he knew how to dress." I tossed her comments in my mental trash can and refused to be sucker punched. The boleros at the pier in Old San Juan after dinner allowed her a venue to uncover lost treasures. Peering out at Cataño across the bay, she lamented a potpourri of comments about opportunities stolen from her youth as we stood on El Malecón. A full moon and a welcome breeze provided serenity as we chatted until after midnight. Heading back, we strolled lazily without a curfew. I placed my arm down to her shoulder; she took her thumb and inserted it in the belt loop of my pants. I had discovered a lot of love for this woman. Tender exchanges such as these provided me moments to revel in sentiments. Unbeknownst to her, I felt so lucky. We paid the slots a visit. Lo and behold! The girl scored some small pots. She was in casino heaven.

All the joyous free-spiritedness exercised the night before was absent the morning after. The suitcase was sprung open; yesterday's attack on her mother resumed. "Chuito told me I would suffer. I've been a good person," she proclaimed. Lowering the volume on my hearing aids, I entered her room with the appropriate greeting, "La Bendición." Foforito responded, "Que Dios te bendiga." I offered her some Bustelo coffee, her favorite brand, and she nodded her answer. Nothing like a good cup of joe to get the day fueled for adventure. She proceeded as the self-proclaimed martyr. I was starting to feel sorry for my grandmother, Doña Provi (short for Providencia). I never called her Abuela. I think my mother's accounts of abuse from her had something to do with my decision. In any case, Provi was very kind to me. I mean, how many times was Foforito going to throw her under the bus? Now, God forbid if anyone had said anything inflammatory about my grandmother in my mother's presence, it would have been trench warfare!

I reflected on how, during the last ten months of Provi's life in a vegetative state, she was cared for by the very person she had constantly abused as a child. That was some scary shit, there. As Foforito's venomous rant amplified, I optimistically entertained high hopes for forgiveness. Mistakenly, I had felt that being able to uncover those belittling insults and acrid episodes of maltreatment would allow my mother, in some way, to reconcile and at least contemplate closure. *We need to bury hatchets in order to travel lightly into the hereafter. However, I'm not suggesting that we forget where we dug the hole.*

There was enough resentment-of-mother juice to go around. From time to time, I harbored some hard feelings towards my mother, as, I suppose she had harbored some towards me. I never appreciated her heavy-handed methods of parenting, to say nothing of her intrusiveness into my relationships. My complaint list was long when I thought about it. *Were mom's offenses anywhere near as diabolical as Provi's? Was I trying to arrange a pity party? Of course not! Of course not.*

I had taken to revisiting my father's wisdom. Frequently he would say, "Grudges corral your liberties. They're a heavy load as one tries to navigate the maze of life." Marching on with that disjointed loyalty, I started examining my personal grudges toward the woman who delivered me. I wrestled with the intrusive behavior that corralled my liberties, but in no way had they equaled the reform-school tactics that left life-long scars on my mother's physical and emotional development. Although my nurturer had been a firm disciplinarian, a drill sergeant, her disciplinary tactics were without berating or belittling of our advancement. Nor do I recall being marched to a woodshed for her to get her point across in wicked ways.

Foforito was never a patient person. One had to grasp her example pronto or risk the chancletazo invasion. Those slippers traveled like boomerangs and always found their target. I must admit the woman was good in her heyday. But we, her sons, developed our own defense mechanisms. Christmas gifts became feather-fluffy slippers to replace those house shoes that had the hard-ass soles. I always got a big kick out of watching feathers flying all over the place; she was as fast as the legendary Buddy Rich was on the drums. Addressing these issues will go a long way when my closure becomes a reality. I presumed undressing emotional layers would be a proper starting point.

One morning Foforito awakened, with boxing gloves on and laced. I wasn't sure who her early-morning opponent was, but I didn't want to fight and would rather have countered with calm. I listened to Foforito's "fight talk" and prepared to defend myself. She was complaining about Angel Luis, Doña Lydia's boyfriend, who had visited a few days before. He was kind and he was generous; but he could be obnoxious. Foforito had barked into his ear, "They're all leaches." She enjoyed mocking others' flaws; in doing so, she avoided examining her own. Apparently Angel Luis had become a temporary comrad. *Aha!* Foforito's boxing blows weren't aimed at Angel Luis nor me, at least not this time. *Duck; retreat.* In the name of peace, I agreed with my mother's analysis…, "leaches." As had been shown in her interactions with Denise, and others, Foforito's slanderous opinion was about anyone, who offered me affection. She disliked anyone who dared get wedged between us; they were the enemy. I suspected that I'd become Chuito in her mind. Constantly, she reminded me of my likeness to him and would chirp, "even your attitude..."

I knew her jealousy had been a challenge for my dad; she'd always been one to protect her interests. In this case, her security blanket—me—was paramount. So, dressed in puritan white, she slung mud with reckless abandon. It was a beautiful day for the beach, and we could have some burgers at El Hamburguero, the best greasy-spoon hamburger joint on the island; she unlaced the gloves. Food that extinguished her cravings was usually a good selling point. First, she had to exercise her perfectionist ways by organizing her room and her possessions. Foforito still had skates under those slippers, but her inner world could easily sidetrack her focus.

Escambrón, the beach at the foot of Old San Juan was close by and safe. I was able to manage La Vieja's whereabouts in that quaint family environment. There was an abundance of foliage and clusters of erect palm trees. It was a weekday, so we could choose seating arrangements without having to compromise. Under a shady tree in close proximity to the ladies' room, yet enough away from the stench was just right.

A clear sky with vacationing clouds and a welcoming breeze was the ideal backdrop for the journey's purpose, eats and beach. The aqua-blue sea called me into the mix where I clumsily approached and submerged myself. I entertained the fantasy of bottling the moment so I could preserve the feeling attached to it. A glance at my honey showed Foforito struggling to get out of her seat; she needed to relieve herself immediately. As I was making my way, a lady offered to assist her. I appreciated the gesture and reached into my bag for a fresh diaper. I had learned to be mindful to prevent diaper rash, which could cause infection of private parts, especially to those of advanced age, so I also had some sanitizing wipes. Jokingly, I told the lady I had forgotten suspenders for the diaper. We had a good little chuckle at Foforito's expense, and since she couldn't hear, she joined in the laughter, oblivious to what had been said.

The diapering mission completed, I thanked my volunteer assistant and turned to address my writing pangs as I grabbed my pen and scribbled notes on my pad. My flow had gotten interrupted by my frail mom's relief episode. Meanwhile, she had reached for her prayer books, squinting into them as if she was unable to decipher the lettering. Foforito had little to no schooling, so the text she recited was from memory. She had mastered the content from repetition. I found it commendable that, with limited resources, she had been able to retain that information and recite it all flawlessly. I lent her my reading glasses and planted a kiss on her crown. She welcomed the affection I heaped on her and claimed the glasses were perfect for her needs. A lonely procession back to the water's edge had me contemplative on the realm of possibilities had she been provided a formal education, given the skills she had mastered while unlettered.

As promised, we had lunch at El Hamburguer, but only after I had had my fill of the beach. It had been difficult removing myself from the activities that entertained me in the seaside setting. The Capitol, gleaming in the distance, was complimented by La Fortaleza, majestic in its own right. A cruise ship was making its way to port and the San

Juan atmosphere was festive; after all, tourism is a lifeline for Puerto Rican economy. Most intriguing were the surfers who rode on waves to the shore, repeating the act like a ritual. I couldn't fathom the adrenaline that flowed for them out there flirting with the elements. It must have been thrilling, but was not part of my bucket list, at least not in this lifetime. I got a kick out of Foforito at the hamburger joint, as she devoured the burger and fries and let out a pleasurable groan. A big ketchup smile broadened from cheek to cheek and she quickly wiped herself clean before I was able to have a Kodak moment.

The day had taken a toll on my girl, but I needed to have her walk a bit so that night's slumber would be lengthy and without incident. La Vieja had worn me down and then asked for some ice cream; just like that. The thought of fueling her with a sugar rush scared me. At day's end, I had come to realize that at some juncture in my life, I would reflect on these moments with gratitude in my heart for allowing myself to be part of her last go-around in her place of origin. I relented and gave in to her fetish.

Getting an early jump on the trip to Benny and Eloisa's allowed time for me to do some sun-worshipping and still get back with time enough to prepare to go to the concert with Pete and Blanca. Placing my mother in safe hands had me in the position to let my hair down—well, figuratively—, since my locks had abandoned me over the past few years, and those that remained were converting in color. Jokingly, La Vieja and I teased each other about the white hair we each had sprouted.

At times, I felt that the constant stress of caregiving could sink my outlook. I would reevaluate my posture once

I'd achieved my goal, which was yet to be determined. Becoming familiar with the mountains' twists and curves, I drove with less caution and more adventure in mind. Foforito was excited at the thought of spending some bonding time with siblings, who had, even at a distance, maintained an alliance.

True to her fashion, she was a loud chatterbox for the duration of the trip. This seemed a logical defense mechanism for her to avoid addressing her need for hearing aids. Meanwhile, my vocal cords had been compromised because of her vanity. On the other hand, the thought of forcing her to get them and then constantly having to locate misplaced hearing aids was nightmarish.

After dropping Foforito off and following a quick fix at the beach, a shower and some grooming, then finally heading for Pete and Blanca's crib. Delaney (Pete's real name), my confidant since before we were of legal drinking age, welcomed me with a glass of wine. Despite distance, Pete and I had remained friends since 1964. Catching up and reflecting over vintage music put us in a nostalgic frame of mind. It was always a kick connecting, making a moment happen. The wine and appetizers allowed me to shed a load off my shoulders, if only for a few hours. Comfortably welded to the lounge chair on the patio, the weight of responsibility was being replaced with seasoned friendship and entertainment plans. It also helped that I was free of driving duties.

At an appropriate stage of social discourse in his life, my father knew the importance of friendship and the fellowship feelings associated with male bonding. In turn, I embraced the importance of this juncture. Pete and

Blanca seemed to be in harmony with each other, and there was genuine appreciation for their merriment.

Upon reflection, I realized that my mother had no such bonds. From birth, her life had been saturated with responsibility that didn't afford her friendships. That is not to say she wasn't a social animal, but her confidantes were relegated to neighbors and family. Outside of those inner circles, my mother never ventured beyond her specific social circumference. At times, I imagined that she had a disdain for those who just made it a point to enjoy their lives but frolicked overboard, by her standards. She was consumed with, and critical of, others' liberties, a conditioning which I assessed was brought on by the burdens of servitude. In reflection, I reviewed the dwindling episodes of her life, the trips we'd taken and the places that travel had allowed us to view. We've gone everywhere from Broadway performances to cruises in from the Caribbean to Central America and all sorts of adventures in between. How giddy she'd felt witnessing things once so alien to her. I imagined further the realm of possibilities had she been afforded proper schooling and the generosity of a gentle upbringing.

Listening to some R & B with Pete, we began recollecting our heydays. I couldn't help feeling a little resentment that Foforito had always reined in our liberties and scrutinized our choices. Her "above and beyond" protection caused many rifts which stifled our quest for balance in our personal relationships. I guess it was her way of protecting her interests. But it was always at the expense of those who showed affection or shared an involvement.

I also witnessed and was frightened by Foforito's bigoted views when a woman (potential love interest) introduced into the mix had a complexion darker than her own. Looking back, I speculated Foforito must have felt cursed, because each of her three sons married women whose complexions varied from black to high yellow. The silver lining, if one should be considered, was that Foforito eventually came around and embraced those she had demonized. The devastation she heaped on others and the offenses she tattooed on those we had chosen to love remained a point of contention. I took a sip of wine and realigned my thoughts. The melancholy feeling was replaced by the thought that the Los Van Van concert was moments in the waiting.

Outstanding! The Los Van Van concert was everything advertised and then some. Attending it became a springboard for things that followed, and my ability to confront them. As we age, I discovered, we embrace the importance of a point in time when something memorable occurs; more so than we would have known how to do in our carefree youth.

As one who engages in ATS (active tongue syndrome) on both literal and metaphorical levels, I began savoring moments like forbidden candy. Whatever future cavities there might be would be a small price to pay for the sweet things that entertained my current indulgences.

Since I wasn't going to Naranjito until the following evening, another beach escape would be available without challenge. The bounce in my walk was telling; my body felt light, carefree, almost intoxicated. I could read, write, dive, and scan my surroundings without those dark clouds of caretaking responsibility. "Duty free" had taken on a new meaning, and it felt wonderful. Young energetic bodies were moving about celebrating their tender years. Their picture-perfect anatomy livened my past; it was a Juicy Fruit moment. Luckily, my shades camouflaged the focused attraction. I laughed inwardly, tickled at the thought. It was so therapeutic entertaining snapshots from my youth and the exploits which made them memorable. Reality told me that soon I'd be reacquainted with the mission at hand, and at that juncture it would be okay.

The radio music on my way back to the countryside was informative company, framing the landscape with rhythm and meaningful verse. Song after song storytelling accounts in the lyrics poetically connected dots, both complex and simplistic. The road was becoming friendly, its curves seductive and enticing; the unknown was finally less menacing at each bend. I was beginning to feel as if the journey was taking on a life that had more to do with self-discovery than with allegiance to Foforito's original mission. Before I realized it, I was at the entrance to Benny's home. There a fixed-link fence connected me to the steps leading to his verandah and the hammocks which laced around like delicate embroidery. He startled me, coming from the rear with fish food for his goldfish that frolicked under the miniature bridge I had just crossed. After the bloated fish had their fill, he mentioned it was his turn for some grub. The aroma of the Chinese food we had purchased, caused us to keep the windows down for the remainder of our ride to Comerio. As we got closer to Eloisa's home an eerie feeling took hold of me. The unexpected was the norm when Foforito was in the equation.

Even at a distance I could hear her agitated conversation with herself. How quickly I could become deflated never ceased to amaze me. I felt for Eloisa; after all, she had her hands full with Tomás and Tomásito. Foforito was complaining about unaccountable garments, the ones she had made by hand and sacrificed to prepare for herself. At times, I would have liked to have slipped my mother a mickey, but the thought of her falling frightened me. So that day she was a prophet of doom: cranky, accusing, and unappreciative. The phantom threads were scattered atop a bed as the heap inside her mind kept unraveling. When she felt my presence, Foforito started sobbing and complaining simultaneously. I didn't want to entertain her drift but asked for her blessings instead.

Eloisa, acknowledging my plight, communicated silently to me with her eyebrows and breathed a sigh of relief that I had arrived to reclaim my duty. No longer deputized to tend a new group of liabilities, she exhaled. She hugged me in a way that energized my will for moving forward. It was a welcomed moment that clung to me in a mystical way.

Tomásito had become the usual suspect. It was interesting that whoever Foforito picked on to blame were vulnerable or unable to defend themselves. I gathered her belongings, thanked everyone for their assistance, and made plans to return at another date for a family gathering. The ride back was pepper sprayed with condescending remarks. She seemed to undermine the good intentions that had been presented. I found the behavior repulsive and draining; I wouldn't allow Foforito to evaporate my good downtime that had taken place in her absence. Plain and simple, I wouldn't bump heads with a ninety-one-year-old stubborn mule. *Now, how would I reprimand my mother when she started her antics? Delicately* was the word that came to mind.

The trip back to Benny's had become recognizable. Not feeling intimidated by the road allowed me a better view of the countryside and what it had to offer. A glance at the rearview mirror captured Foforito soaking up remnants of her yesteryears. The approach to Benny's hacienda reminded me of the TV show, *Bonanza*; I imagined the opening jingle was announcing our arrival. The lushness and inescapable beauty was punctuated by the mammoth mango tree (my grandmother, Doña Provi, had planted it when *she* was a child) blooming in the rear and the huge avocado tree that guarded the entrance. All was testament to his toil. With the day's activities already becoming memories, I started my descent to my pillowed landing strip. Benny headed for his quarters as we parted company for the night.

Foforito began her ritual of blame, rehashing the theft of garments that had never been packed. Her deaf ears filtered out the click-clack clatter of chancletas marching neurotically into the night as they competed with the coquí lullabies. I closed my door knowing that her protests would dissipate soon enough. At times like those, I felt comfortable with my hearing loss, even though it had shortchanged my ability to be social.

The day of our family gathering showed promise as the weather was generous with its offerings. My cousins arrived. Teresita, with her son, Juan Carlos; Miguel, with his wife Blanca; and Luisa, their mother and my mother's partner in crime from back in the day. Isaura, Benny, Eloisa, Tomás, Tomásito, Foforito and I rounded out a circle of generational personalities. I could never comprehend how everyone could be talking simultaneously, with increasing velocity and volume, yet, honestly digest the conversations at hand, even though I had grown up knowing that gift to be innate in Puerto Ricans. The long-winded discourse reaches a crescendo, catches a breath and resumes without skipping a beat. Incredible. Come to think about it, I guess that's how it goes in most big family gatherings.

I started capturing the moment on camera, while all the animated folks jockeyed for the best position in what were supposed to be candid shots. As platforms for expression were established, gossip entered the mix. I supposed since we rarely gathered, everybody had a need to spill their guts. Eloisa had prepared a feast fit for kings and queens and yappers. Traditional homemade food—arroz con gandules to pasteles to pulpo salad—was and is always a blessing to my belly. With food aplenty, I filled my tank to the max. Coffee, pastries, and of course, clandestine rum, made all the silly jokes actually laughable. It was an outright fun fest. Naturally, no gathering would be complete without the group pictures.

La Vieja was in her element as the eldest in the circle. She received the baton willingly. A light filtered past the ornamental stone wall that separated neighbors. Delicate rays framed the family portrait perfectly, with Foforito as the central figure. The adulation had her in a euphoric state. Her boat may have been taking in too much water, but at the moment she was rowing royally.

Family history became the priority topic. Felito, Teresa, Benjamín, and Alberto had passed on. But those characters were re-birthed with remembrances highlighting their youth through the shared bonding of those present. The remaining eleven siblings were aging, some not gracefully.

Out of the blue, the expected bomb exploded as my mother made the most inappropriate comments about me and her financial circumstances and living arrangements. She started saying that I'm dependent on her financially. Reader, let me tell you… Her monthly stipend barely covered her needs. And when she hit the casinos, she wound up in the red. She was also oblivious to her assets, which had gradually dwindled as they paid for her out of pocket expenses, this trip being a case in point. In my defense, I cracked, "The casinos have retained her bloomers as collateral for her debts." Trying to make light of her ill-conceived comments, I didn't feel a need to defend or answer away her provocative account of her accounts. Yet, it irked me when she descended to mudslinging. Once we had a moment, Eloisa whispered in my ear that she knew better than what had been said. "You're a good son. Don't ever forget that."

At day's end, the prolonged Puerto Rican goodbyes took their course. Phone numbers which we would probably never USE were exchanged. Hugs and kisses were repeated. Grapefruits and other homegrown produce were offered as parting gifts. I made a financial contribution to Eloisa. Our final hug was an intimate acknowledgement of the mutual hardships that she and I each had undertaken. Foforito started to tear up as we began the road trip back to Benny's home. The emotional gathering had us all drained and ready for the sack. Surprisingly, Foforito was first to go to sleep once we got to Benny's house. Whereas, usually

I had to sleep with one eye open, this night Foforito's cooperation allowed both of my eyes to rest.

Morning dewdrops accompanied me as I made my way to the mango tree full of itself. The manicured landscape had become a chore for Benny, then, well into his eighties. He had highlighted the grounds with decorative concrete molds and found objects. I was gaining a better understanding of the source of my creative talents; they were in the genes. I saw Benny under a bed of orchids located in a shady section. The canopy provided a filter to allow just enough sunlight for their growth. As we chatted, he shared that his intention was to sell the property. The maintenance had become too much for him to handle. What was once therapeutic was now a burden. My heart sank at the thought; after all, his Ponderosa was as close as one could come to heaven. Sadly, I understood not only the upkeep, but the isolation, the ramifications of falling ill, and the inevitable aging process were significant challenges which contributed to his decision to sell. Foforito appeared and immediately tried unsuccessfully to wrap her arms around Benny. I commented that either she had short arms or he needed to stay away from the tripe soup. With that said, we got into the car, and you guessed it... headed straight to the greasy spoon.

An invasion of motorcycles had descended on the countryside. The deafening sounds of revving motorcycles had Benny grumbling. Stuck in traffic, I asked one of the cyclists if he could give my mother and uncle a lift to the restaurant. The light-hearted humor allowed Benny to unwind a bit, and soon enough a familiar breakfast was being served. I again urged my mama to be mindful with her order, and she complied. My next thought was, *Now, how do we navigate the maze of wild two wheelers?* Foforito was already confronting the band of cyclists, who were surprisingly (my prejudice) civil. They asked her for her blessings and provided us an escort out of town. In turn, my Foforito, high-fived some of the members. I thought she might become an honorary affiliate with a leather jacket and all, maybe even some tattoos, but that thought was short-lived. The trip back to Benny's was lengthy as the cyclists dominated the roads and the watering holes along the way. The encounter with the motorcycles turned into an adventure, and it was a pleasant surprise to see my lady so into the moment. After prying, Benny grudgingly admitted to having done some chest pounding in his youth. People tend to conveniently forget, as if we could erase our own footprints on the roads we've traveled.

A temporary stop to drop off Benny had my mother rushing to the toilet. Food cut through her like Drano. She regrouped, and like a tough biker, got back on the road—once we did the prolonged Puerto Rican goodbye thing.

We connected with Doña Lydia and her mate Angel Luis. My mother's disabled ears interpreted what people said as an affront. Any remarks, comments, or conversations could fuel her insecurities. She'd lash out wretchedly, especially when she didn't care for an individual to begin with. In this case, Angel Luis was the villain. I left to get some pizza as Doña Lydia kept the peace.

I made a point of getting my girl some soup for her unhinged stomach. When I returned, she saw the pizza and said she couldn't eat that. I presented the soup; she flipped a switch and wanted the pizza. Since I was tired from engaging with her earlier that day at Benny's, I denied her the slice. She had a meltdown and refused to budge from either her demands or from the kitchen. She pouted and cried, but when the hunger pangs kicked in, she ate the soup.

Later, even though she had eaten the soup, Foforito remained predictably headstrong and even started losing it. She adamantly resented the fact that I had denied her a slice. But, wait! After I went to sleep, she pillaged the fridge. During her raid, she devoured Ice cream, yogurt, some potato chips, a piece of cheese, and yes, a slice of pepperoni pizza.

It occurred to me that an aged brat was my consolation prize for not having a bunch of mischievous children. Needless to say, I was relieved that despite the fact Foforito had gobbled up that midnight mis-menu without my knowledge or blessings, and against my wishes,— except the yogurt, maybe—the refrigerator bandit had no messy eruptions the next day.

Few and far between were opportunities to enjoy traditional dishes prepared by those who had honed their trade in the kitchen. So, when Doña Lydia extended an invitation for some home cooking at Angel Luis's farm, we accepted without any hesitation. The fried fish and the viandas put me in a state of ecstasy. Foforito always became animated when in a countryside environment. As a bonus, Angel's farm provided her a springboard to her youth. The gandules bush, oregano, and other offerings from the fields were in abundance.

She managed the trek up the steep incline with Angel Luis, and started plucking, picking, and stripping the farm of its donations. She was incredibly knowledgeable when it came to the pulse of agriculture and raising livestock. It was the common thread that hitched those two earthbound farmhands. They volleyed their intrinsic understanding of earthly contributions, and their grounded beliefs and practices on the matter. Angel prepared a produce package of farm goods and was officially off the shit list. After all, he had been very generous with the yield of his field. He also committed to providing us a batch of items upon our departure from the island. As we descended to the house Foforito whispered to me, "He's not really a bad guy, just a bit repugnant." Mi vieja could hand out accolades and daggers in the same breath; she was good that way. I'd come to understand that my mother was a person with good intentions wrapped in rough edges. I was learning how to shed some of the rough edges I had ingested by repetition. Shedding that inheritance lightened my spirit

Back at the house, Foforito started rattling off the list of the abuses Doña Provi would heap on her after a day of toiling and rearing. According to modern public laws, my grandmother would have done some serious time for her methods of discipline. Returning to her origins triggered a past that had been extremely unkind to Foforito. The lack of acknowledgement by her own siblings still clawed away without resolution. Tattooed in her redundant memory, her conscience wreaked of unresolved issues that, in all likelihood, could recur at a moment's notice. The damage was obvious and etched into her contorted explanation of that warped period.

Angel Luis started defending my grandmother's heavy-handed ways as, "just the way things were back then."

Was that supposed to excuse the behavior and liberate the trauma? I wasn't buying it. "So was slavery," I chirped sarcastically, rebutting his opinion. "'That was just the way things were doesn't cut away at the emotional plight my mother inherited," I interjected in defense of Foforito.

"Hey," he spouted, "look, you became a good by-product of the strict practices that existed back then." Angel Luis kept jumping back to the top of that shit list; in this case, mine. Foforito, being hearing impaired, hadn't quite made out his trivializing remarks.

I thought she had become the better person despite the indecent assaults bestowed on her as the eldest female sibling of fifteen children. That merciless period had defined her youth, molded her future and hampered her potential. Triumphantly, my mother's rebellious spirit and inner resolve had plowed forward. Her fortitude in moments of uncertainty or despair had guided her warrior's spirit. As we headed back to Doña Lydia's abode with renewed vigor I began to reconfigure my appreciation for my mother's make-up.

The next day Foforito dove into her suitcase, conducting inventory of the wardrobe of handmade garments which showcased her talent. According to her, things were missing. Watching Foforito dig for "missing" garments here in Puerto Rico, brought to mind a search and blame episode that had occurred back in New Jersey, months ago. Al had sent Foforito a hobby, needlepoint tapestry to embroider. "Where is the needlepoint?", she had whined while searching aimlessly in her bedroom area in my house. "What will Al think?" Her unhinged world was crumbling; she was hyperventilating. Between breaths, she claimed, "El diablo sabe más por viejo que por diablo." Although her acting skills were honed, I was becoming better able to identify and separate what was real from what was imagined. So, I had dismissed her end-of-the-world drama, "We'll find it, relax." Realizing that I wasn't taking the bait, Foforito collected herself, a small victory for me, a then evolving caretaker. I had lied and told her Al called asking for her, and he had said not to worry about the tapestry. I reflected on the similarities of Foforito's bizarre behavior before and during this trip.

So, here we were at Doña Lydia's, preparing to return to New Jersey—después, quioscos y fincas y familia. When had these words written themselves into my dictionary? This journey had emerged as search and discovery for roots of Foforito's life story. Her jealousy, born of mistreatment, wrapped in loss and confusion, came with vocabulary... dementia, Alzheimer's, onset.

Foforito had become so clingy it startled me. Our trip, like the winding roads in Barranquitas, had been telling. It had announced to her family her personal forfeiture of time which couldn't be reclaimed. It awakened the reality of difficult decisions that would have to be made. Reviewing the similarities of Foforito's bizarre behavior before and during this trip helped me to assemble the pieces of my own tapestry. I recalled that I had empathized with my brother when he had defended his family against Foforito's accusations about missing items. Here I was in the same place, accused. I was the whipping boy, and Foforito was her mother. The unresolved issues Foforito had with her mother, Doña Provi, had a pit bull's grip on my mother's sense of right and wrong and being a victim. The longer the hold, the more crippling and crushing it became. Conscience is a tricky fella, and I was an emotional creature. Those scrambled scruples had me twisted into a pretzel. I sensed Foforito was well-aware of that.

When I felt suffocated, I tried to summon the defiance that seemed to come to Al so easily; but not as easily to me. I wrestled with anguish that was like an octopus.

How would I solve a particular problem?

Who would help me?

What would Foforito say and do?

What would others say about the choices I made—

by myself?

I had to become better able to execute a persuasive resolve and stay the course. Soon, I realized it was unnecessary to seek anyone's blessings or approval for the actions I took. Foforito was sliding down to the dark side of wonderland. I accepted that she might require medication to control her bouts with anxiety. If a prescription for it were attainable, it could go a long way towards securing some "normalcy" in our remaining time together. Simultaneously, I was apprehensive that medication that sedated her could bear undesired consequences. The Catch-22 was apparent at every turn. I decided that if I carefully approached the curves along the way, I'd be better prepared to deal with what lurked around the bend. Hopefully, when she transitioned, the understanding would be that I had done all I could have done for her. I sensed Foforito was well-aware of that, also. I released caring what anyone else thought of the matters at hand.

On the cusp of ninety-two, La Vieja was still physically perky and fluid. I thanked her God for such fortitude.

Nap time. Immediately as my head hit the pillow, questions arose that brought to light realistic concerns. The wear and tear of caregiving continued to impair my vision. Personally, I viewed the windows of opportunity dwindling for myself. I felt like the aged banana—bruised and on the verge of becoming manure. Time, it seemed, had been in a fast-forward position, entertaining a dark abyss. *Who will care for me?* I asked myself. The nursing facilities were nauseating. *Someday, will someone discover me by the stench of decay?* I settled into a sinkhole, the seasons were slipping away, and these images placed me in a funk. *How could I liberate my incarcerated adventures?* The answer to that remained a mystery as I towel-wiped my perspiration mixed with leftover saltwater yet to be properly washed away. Hopefully, having to deal with my own elder care details would be years away. Jumping to attention, I headed to the shower, encouraged that I could wash the disturbing thoughts into the tub, out to the gutter.

As the pelting shower became a tonic, my thoughts turned to Foforito. She had never allowed her memory loss or other afflictions to handicap her outlook. Her plow-forward mindset had always been commendable. At her age she still made her bed, swept the floor, washed dishes, dusted, cleaned, and even juiced oranges the old-fashioned way, with a spoon. *She didn't dwell on her demise, so why should I?* At the end of the day, why engage the inevitable, if it's inevitable? *Take advantage of the moment at hand* became my mantra.

Valentine's Day, like Presidents' Day, like all the other

commercial holidays, baffled me. A touch of envy came to surface as I witnessed couples entwined, in the moment. Foforito became my date by default. We headed to Isla Verde for dinner, and a sense of privilege stirred me. Watching her across the red tablecloth in her polyester outfit, she observed the menu with a regal presence. I wondered about her comprehension of the menu. Foforito had not been afforded a basic education; I knew she could not read the words. Thinking about how my mother had been mishandled and deprived as a child was not a favorable appetizer. I leaned in closer as she closed the meaningless paper and asked me what I was having. An overhead light haloed her well-groomed locks. A lump rose as I tried to put into words what I'd been reviewing in my gut. Getting a grip on my emotions, I asked her what she would like to eat, and proceeded to read the menu to her. I already knew her choice would be either shrimp or chicken. Across the table, the wrinkled pages of her life, apparent on her face, were so telling and tender. Her life had been saturated with personal loss, heart ache, and unwanted duty.

I saw my mother, a battle-tested, imposing elder, archiving her remembrances as she conveyed missing my father on a day reserved for lovers. He had provided her affection without limitations, and she still welcomed the memory of his being, thirty years after his passing. I placed the order and told her that at present she was stuck with me. With a sigh she replied, "At least you look alike."

Dessert and a demitasse cup of coffee punctuated the moment. As we got ready to leave the restaurant, she wrapped her small frail limbs around my waist and thanked me for being. On the way out, I paused at the bar; a shot of Remy, in the name of the old man, heated my heart. Foforito nodded her approval. Heading towards the car I asked if she would like to try her luck with the one-armed bandits. To my surprise she declined, claiming the day had worn her.

Foforito slipped into her bata, removed her false teeth and placed them in a glass, and then made a beeline for the bed. She never had problems hitting the sack; accordingly, that evening she was anchored to the mattress and soundly sleeping in minutes.

Pete called, inviting me to a dance. I felt a little torn, like a kid wanting to sneak out a window to hang with friends. Usually guilt and stress played hardball against me leaving Foforito. I felt guilt for going, and stress about the unforeseen upon my return. That evening, having sipped three black Russian cocktails, helped me strip away some of my inhibitions. It's fair to say I had become socially dysfunctional lately. Magically, the music and the moment allowed me to let my guard down. I rationalized that in a few days we'd be headed back north to the cold, and the unwelcome task of shoveling snow.

A slow drive from the dance had me filled with gratitude; these last few weeks had been gutsy and revealing. I felt a sense of accomplishment for having facilitated Foforito's request to become a reality. Finally, I looked in on her in the quarters she had occupied for the past two weeks; hours later she had remained anchored in the same position. I exhaled and headed down the hall dignified, tanned, relieved, and eager to hug my pillow.

The journey had dwindled to a precious few days;

the goals had been met, and the remaining time on that calendar of events were simply formalities. I negotiated a day at the beach in exchange for a last visit to Eloisa's home. Looking ahead, I shivered at the thought that snow awaited; my back moaned as the weather reports confirmed my fears.

On our next-to-last day in sun paradise, I packed my swim wear, and got La Vieja ready for a final expedition to the welcoming waves of the beach in Isle Verde. To my surprise, Foforito was very accommodating. She appeared to be in a playful mood, so I rolled with that, allowing her to roam about at the beach collecting shells and stones. A mischievous wave unsettled her, and she laughed nervously as she gathered herself. As a non-swimmer and fearful of the ocean currents, she became guarded. Easing her fears, I encouraged her to enter as far as she wanted as I held her arm supportively. "The ocean is medicinal; let me wet your legs." Her tense stance evaporated as the waters' warmth and the shifting sand beneath her feet provided a healing calm. The "Sea Dance" was repeated a few times encouraging some unfounded inhibitions to dissipate. That was groundbreaking for her, since her childhood had been absent of these simple pleasures. Immediately after her stolen childhood, she had married, and both inherited and birthed a total of six children and never turned back, not even for a dip in the ocean.

Puerto Ricans were celebrating Presidents' Day, which I found a bit odd since they couldn't vote for the people who would send their children to war. Foforito sat back on her beach chair under the shade of festive palm trees as a persistent breeze lulled her to catch some zzzs. The needle, multicolored-threads, and the prayer books littered her bata. The sound of the ocean and the persistent breezes lulled her to sleep, claiming victory from their wrestling match with her. I began massaging my feet with the pebbles at the ocean's edge; it was a tender moment punctuated by intimate inner groans.

Watching parents being mindful had me peer at my Mami with her wandering ways. I started tickling her ear with a branch. She awakened, annoyed, and in a demanding tone bellowed, "Hey! Stop it, man." I got a kick from her animated outbursts. Slowly, I became somber at the thought that I never witnessed my mother being frolicsome. For reasons unknown to me, Foforito never owned a bathing suit. In her lifetime, she had gone from rearing her mother's responsibilities, to her own term of motherhood to caretaking, to being cared for. Her timeline leapfrogged from birth to obligation without landing in the sandbox of her childhood. Just as expected, she shook her head as she viewed some young girls in bikinis, g-strings, and thongs. "What is this world coming to?" she mumbled. Personally, I was glad they were in the world and that she had brought them to my attention.

With stage-worthy exaggeration of hunger pains, Foforito claimed anew that I was starving her to death. I suggested a number of local places where we could indulge that discomfort. Bebo's, her choice, was conveniently on the way back to the house. The seasoned rotisserie chicken and boiled batatas we ate were finger-licking. Our greasy faces were telling, as a mound of napkins sopped up the greasy evidence that had us butt-heavy on the outdoor benches. During our one month visit to Puerto

Rico, we had eaten our way through countryside menus that had been delicious and borderline criminal. Yes, our meal choices had contained bad cholesterol and other nutrition no-nos. Admittedly, we had indulged in the easy evils of tasty food. 'Choice' was the operative word here, and we were happy and satisfied with ours. Certainly, a detox regiment was a must upon returning to New Jersey. It was time to move on. In the car I strapped the seatbelt around her emerging belly to secure my contented girl, assumed chauffer position and started creating the to-do list in my head.

Once we returned to Doña Lydia's house, the first thing on my to-do list was to organize and coordinate for our journey back home. Anticipating the packing drama, I reinforced the new pre-flight security rules. "Finish packing so I can deposit our luggage at the airport." I laughed at the nonsense I made up just to make the transition seamless. Carefully I policed her carry-on items, making sure needles, scissors or any sharp objects were removed. Exhausted, she decided to catnap, which afforded me a moment to fasten my own loose ends. I was gleeful that the jumbled pieces were falling into place, creating a pre-calm as we prepared for what would undoubtedly include stops in Naranjito and Comerio, each with an emotional exit on this farewell tour in Puerto Rico.

And so, it began, we made our way along those winding roads which were skirted with nature's lushness welcoming us at every bend. The scene, and the spirit which accompanied it, was a gift for the human eye and for the soul. Benny repeated stories constantly yet managed a different twist in each retelling. Those woven tapestries of storytelling clung like good cholesterol. His entertaining conversations lay the groundwork and stimulated my thoughts for this memoir in the making. The next bend deposited us at Eloisa's porch. As usual, the warm greeting reminded me of my playful dog, Magui, and his excitement even before I had opened the door. The only missing ingredient was the licking. Hugs and kisses were aplenty and well received. Eloisa, as was custom, prepared some food, a poor man's soup-to-nuts, punctuated with strong coffee and dessert. Not to be forgotten was the bootlegged alcohol as a nightcap.

Again, we photo-posed awkwardly and made the requisite silly statements to provoke laughter. The camera captured some vintage moments as we braced for the never-ending Puerto Rican goodbyes. I glanced at Foforito and saw her emotions braided and telling. I wondered if she viewed this farewell as the last go-round; the last encounter with those who had taken part in her childhood. Those here kept a common bond and identified with her struggles, yet more importantly, they secured her contributions as the matriarch of the Morales clan.

As usual, Foforito became a tangled, passionate mess. Selfishly, I turned away, connecting to my own sentiments, which, at the moment, were brittle and unsettled. As was my choice, I reserved the last hug for Eloisa. Without flinching, she had remained a force in the face of adversity. I prayed for her and the cross she carried; her fortitude filled my heart. Her words of encouragement resonated as they empowered my purpose. I glanced in the rearview mirror, which framed the fading, waving hands that had been welcoming in receiving us and were heartfelt in saying goodbye.

The slow procession out of Comerio left behind a trail of tears; a damp wind ruffled my girl's hair, and she gazed out into the bends. The landscape was telling as our melancholy eyes looked to the future and reviewed the past. I sensed that Foforito was well aware of what lay ahead. Her declining health and limited movements were accompanied by a fuzzy outlook, which of late couldn't separate what was real from what was imagined. The ride back was somber as we pulled up to Benny's abode in Naranjito. Now, in this leisurely period of his life, Benny no longer had the stamina or the finances to upkeep the house on the hill. His legs concerned me; they were swollen, discolored, and frequently required being raised while he was horizontal. Sensitivity to sun rays, caused raw and peeling blotches on his scalp and face; yet, he refused to a wear hat.

My mother, Benny, and Alberto were joined at the hip, pioneers carving a path for the remaining siblings who had landed on cotton cushions. These siblings reluctantly landing on the mainland paved the road for the Morales migration to the States. I had witnessed Benny, a proud man with guarded feelings who once scolding me for crying over "nonsense" as he had bid my father farewell when my parents had moved to California, bawling as he embraced Chuito in his wheelchair. I guess Benny knew that would be their last moments together.

My father's words resonated. "Men will ultimately be defined by the number of tears they're willing to share." My dad returned home to New York, three months to the day he had left, in a modest coffin and to a wake full of

122

Three of the 15 Morales siblings:
Benny, Foforito and Alberto in their youth August 1944

well-wishers. Benny was front and center, in tears, as we laid my father to rest. He knelt before my old man and poured his sentiments atop his coffin. At that moment, I revisited that statement and its evolution in my life. Benny remained my favorite uncle, one I immensely enjoyed hanging with. I will always be grateful to him for the love that he provided me without reservation.

Alberto, the third link in the migration trek, joined my mother as they became exposed to the trials of servitude. At the time, he was confined to shade due to a skin disorder that left his delicate layers peeling, raw and sensitive to the touch. His outlook had been compromised; his afflictions nudged the dominoes that were very telling of struggle. I had a fondness for Alberto and his wife, Sosa. Married for

Benny, Foforito and Alberto 60 years later in August 2004

sixty years they remained the last bastion of a period that gave rise to the character and conviction of family. They kept to themselves and did not gossip, as they personified humility and decency. I hugged him gingerly as Sosa gave me her blessings before we headed up to Benny's home for our last few moments together.

Swaying in Benny's decorative hammock, I reminisced an occasion in which I had asked my dad if he missed Puerto Rico. His reply had been pointed and telling. He recalled his dad had died when he was very young. Eugenia, my grandmother, left the island in a huff after stabbing a man in the eye with a pair of scissors. She had never revealed the accounts leading up to those actions; however, she confirmed that he deserved the pain he endured. One by one she reclaimed each of her three children as they sailed into the docks of Columbia Street, in the area dubbed as the People's Republic of Brooklyn. Dad was very young; consequently, his memory of Puerto Rico was sketchy at best. It had been a difficult period—foreign country, language barriers; a lengthy list of obstacles. As I pried, he had spoken softly, deliberately, and obviously proud of his cultural background. Yet, while deeply rooted in his ethnicity, during his recollection he conceded that his homeland was an obscure blur in his past; there had been little to cling to. His children, friends and reconstructed family were all here in New York. I knew it saddened his reflection that this was now home. He punctuated our discourse with his declaration of love for his place of origin, adding that I should be equally proud of my cultural connection.

Benny joined me, settling into another hammock. As big brother, mentor, friend and confidant, he, too, had been very distraught when Chuito passed. My connection to Benny was swaddled with history. Foforito and I shared a fondness for Benny which was always uplifting. Each parting whittled away at the inevitable. Saying goodbye was gut-wrenching. We poured a shot of Scotch whisky in Chuito's name to undo the knot in our throats.

A storm of emotions gathered over us as we exited, clouds full of impending doom. Wrapping her arms around Benny, my mother clung to her brother ardently as she unraveled emotionally. Benny reassured her that he would be seeing her soon in New York. Chuito's passing had been a turning point of family gatherings. The once-magic of those reunions were relegated to memory. Our former family traditions were apparently faded and absent at these current events. Time and distance had segregated the once cohesive tribe into groups of strangers. The road back from Benny's home had been littered with scattered visions of that once kindred past.

Tissues absorbing Foforito's moist sentiments gathered on the floor of the rental car around her veiny ankles. They became a paper trail of this rock star's farewell tour, for which I had been the designated driver. She rubbed my arm as we flowed in a deliberate cadence with the curves along the countryside that once had been the very classroom which shaped her moral fiber. Quivering, Foforito thanked me for allowing her moments well spent. In turn, I thanked her for allowing me that privilege. A silence filled our vehicle, interrupted only occasionally by a whistling wind that penetrated a crack in the passenger window. Foforito inspected the blurred images as she reviewed the circumstances that applied to the moment. I tapped her slightly; she got startled and gave me a look of resolution.

The bends along the road were seductively telling. I was transfixed. This twisted, tangled road cocooned scattered emotions, and gathered them like fresh flowers into a basket. My hands clutched the steering wheel which directed this movie-making moment. A mist perfumed the air, each turn, like a wave, bathed me with natural props. The intoxicating lushness was revealing. The filtered air inspired me to recite a poem I'd written twenty years ago. Foforito shifted her attention as I recollected the poem from memory. I knew she couldn't make out the Spanish/English mesh of words which bellowed as I spun my way. I became surprised at myself for recalling those verses and driving onto an unknown path, by all accounts a multi-tasking moment.

> *"I a foolish romantic walk parallel with the sea*
> *The salty breeze ruffles my guayabera*
> *The shoreline is invaded by healing foamy*
> *aqua blue saltwaters*
> *that baptize my blistered chancletaless feet*
> *Sending my body into this unprovoked despojos."*

Her eyes, shiny from sentiment, like marbles, were fixed. They revealed the raw jagged events that defined her past. They also spoke of resolution, confirming to me that this journey had accomplished its intended goals. I was knotted in my gut as I uncoiled my poem. My girl surveyed the cadence with a look of reverence reserved for my dad. I felt elevated that she would bestow me that view. The winding roads of Naranjito were vacant, ours to entertain, and so I stopped reciting for a moment. And then proceeded...

> *"Goose bumps mingle with hair now at attention*
> *Concrete palm trees with cocos blanco*
> *dress up the skirts of Puerto Rico's beaches...*
> *Preaches... teaches the art of oppression of*
> *opulence in a deceitful delicious manner*
>
> *In the rinconcitos y las cuevas carved into the*
> *mountainside you can on occasion run into men*
> *with machetes*
> *Or barefoot children blessing the earth with their*
> *innocence.*

A so called jibarita dressed in the simplicity of a
bata exercises el pilón the aroma of
un sancocho en el fogón dances with scents
of finca offerings from trees and healthy dirt
mesmerizes... paralyzes my crazed cravings.

The wrinkled pages of a viejita's face
speaks of lost treasures as her driftwood
arthritic limbs reach out of the kitchen window
to pluck a prized aguacate to marry with
el sancocho

The thought of colonialism... imperialism...
capitalism... come mierda-isms are erased
by a coro of campesinos en una loma
armed with pavas, cuatros, güiros y maracas
they attack that material mindset with
a spiritual cleansing pure and simplistic.

El sonido de la naturaleza coquí... coquí... coquí
by el King Coquí clings to my ear banks."

I paused again. And then proceeded. I was in my element, and Foforito was coming along for the ride. She couldn't understand my lyrics, but my girl was feeling it, as was I. At that juncture, I recognized that this journey was perhaps the best investment I had ever made with my time in this life.

"The roads to el campo have been buried with
concrete which wear away
eating our fragile emotional souls
as we seek to search out our true identities

A young child climbs a tree with the blood of
Guarionex running through his dormant mind
Moñitos gorditos y sonrisas melladas are in
abundance on a field of cáscaras
y pepitas de quenepas that accompany
children in playful conversation

Los gritos de Lares are deafening
yet fall on so many a deaf ear
En la larga distancia nuestros maestros
Don Pedro... Betances... Hostos... Burgos
se sientan en la mesa de justicia esperando
el sancocho y la rajita de aguacate

The blood and sweat of our true selves
en las salas de la isla
advertised commercialism periodically
interrupts novelas sin caritas
negra y bochinches sin mérito

Material propaganda programs a beautifully
abused island as our consciousness
gets deposited into the banks of Hato Rey
for inflated car loans and high interest rates

The fisherman and the sun rise in unison
one to cast its net
the other to spread its warmth
and bronze our skin

On the air waves of la Isla, Rúben sings
siembra para poder cosechar

The aroma of coffee forever fills my lungs

por donde quiera roosters alarmingly
trumpet in a new virgin day

As I a foolish romantic walk
parallel with the sea
enamorado con los ideales de los maestros

Sentido con las cosas que eran
y frustrado con las cosas que son."

I'm sure Foforito's religious, conservative conditioning would have clashed with my personal views, had she understood the poem that interpreted them. Incidentally, my mother applauded the narrative without question; gifting me an unconditional smile as she rubbed my arm in appreciation. Some moments are markers in one's memory, this, without a doubt was one.

Our journey had awkwardly brought to light issues that I needed to investigate. In the same manner as my mother repeatedly reconfigured the vibrant-colored threads on her tapestry project, I constantly rearranged the words I was writing on the yellow legal pads to suit my intent. Cut from the same cloth as my mother, I had inherited redundancy, an unwanted trait.

In a way, her attention to detail was teaching me the craft of writing. So much was related to the power of recall. The learning curves willed by DNA were reminders that there could be a positive in everything that occurs in our lives if we're sensitive enough to identify and apply them moving forward. I was also made aware that I needed to shed that which I found alien but mimicked as the result of conditioning if it proved destructive and negative.

When we arrived at Lydia's, I escorted Foforito inside with her belongings and deposited her moist tissues into the trash. My sentiments clung internally while I reviewed my own threads of thought and prepared to explore the next learning curve.

The bathroom door was ajar, I could hear her mumbling. She had become increasingly ornery during her morning movements. Because preparation for travel rendered Foforito undone, I had utilized the night before to arrange order in anticipation of chaos. That day's trip had the added importance of irrevocability; she had promoted her plea to take a victory lap. And we did that. As it came to a ripened conclusion, it had reinvigorated her outlook for moving forward.

The contentment in her stride was evident by her greeting from the bathroom sink. Innocently, she had applied BenGay ointment to her toothbrush, and got ready to wash her choppers. Swooping to the rescue in Superman mode, I removed the BenGay from her firm grip and asked, "What are you doing?" She swore at me, and then apologized once she was made aware of the harm that could have resulted. At that point, she was back to wearing out the toilet bowl. Her nervous energy always wreaked bowel havoc, and when coupled with anxiety, it became a two-headed dragon. It followed that her recently reconstructed bionic booty (the specialist surgeon had earned permanent place on my mother's daily prayer list) was sensitive from the diarrhea activity. Locating the Preparation H wipes, I placed them in the basic-necessities bag, which coincidentally was developing a bulge. Extra adult diapers made zipping the bag a challenge. Jokingly, I asked what she would like me to do with the BenGay-laced toothbrush. Her vulgar response was duly noted, as my smile gave way to hearty laughter.

Ironically, Foforito was at a privileged point in time. She punched me in the arm and reminded me that her position as elder wasn't to be played with, even in jest. Her skin on bone attack was bruising, even though she claimed the wallop literally hurt her more than it hurt me. This was a phrase I had heard all too often as a child, and quite frankly, as I rubbed my arm, still made no sense to me.

Angel Luis and Lydia arrived to see us off, collect the keys, and exchange parting hugs. We killed some downtime by watching *Caso Cerrado* a program on the Spanish language station. As we chit-chatted, Angel asked me, "What's your favorite movie for the Oscars?" My reply, *Throw Momma from the Train*, puzzled him since he didn't understand the reference as a joke. I maintained a straight face, as he looked me over awkwardly out of the corner of his eye.

As usual, traveling with an elder had its perks, wheelchair accommodations, first in line, and so on. That was until we ran into the customs bitch from hell. She singled out Foforito, made her stand, ransacked her personal belongings, and then proceeded to touch my mother inappropriately. My maternal bundle of joy, becoming startled, she loudly objected to this kind of search. I was pissed to the point of wanting to smack the nasty excuse for a human being with the letters TSA broadcasted on her jacket. A supervisor stepped in to quell the mounting unrest between me and the woman detaining (and upsetting) my mother.

"I want her name!" Furious, I felt like a bear protecting her cubs. "Arrest me if need be."

I was not leaving until that woman was held accountable for her antics of misguided abuse of power. Meanwhile, my girl, traumatized by the chaos, was yet impressed by my defense of her.

"I want her name," I repeated and was given information to file a complaint, which I had no problem drafting once aboard the flight. Once we were airborne we relaxed and made light of the events that had unsettled us. A few fellow passengers offered their names in case I needed witnesses to verify my accounts of the incident. Foforito slid her hand around mine like a pretzel; my defense of her was not taken lightly as she cuddled up onto me.

Sometimes the purpose of a bad encounter is to transform the negativity of one's outlook and perhaps even the negativity of the encounter. I recalled an incident that occurred when, as children, we lived across the street from the school we attended. At the end of the school day, my mother was watching us cross the street, when a woman clocked my brother with an umbrella. My mother raced down in a huff and began pounding the woman with her own umbrella. Supermom to the rescue! She then put an ass-whipping on my brother, knowing all too well that he wasn't innocent in the scheme of things. We were a handful in our early years, but we were her cubs, and no one laid a hand on her children. She was the only one allowed that form of 'hands-on' rearing; she remained the 'Chancletaso Queen', despite the fluffy slippers fix we had attempted to give her as gift. The TSA episode in the airport helped to galvanize us moving forward; she was reminded that unequivocally I had her back. And, at times, because she was Foforito, she also knowingly abused that belief.

Upon arrival back home, our house was snow-covered, and Foforito was complaining of hunger pains: nothing new. Canned soup and crackers was the menu by default. It was what she commonly labeled 'emergency food.' The house was warm, because I maintain a set temperature during the winter months, even if I am out of town. Compensating two neighborhood kids to shovel the snow saved my back, in a delicate state following our month-long journey to Puerto Rico. I ate soup and crackers and didn't think about unpacking.

The next few days were trying; Foforito wasn't herself moping around the house. I knew something was up when she didn't watch Wheel of Fortune. She refused my suggestion to go to the ER. At last, she relented when she started having a fever and couldn't urinate. She was admitted to the hospital with a urinary tract infection. It was actually a blessing since a storm was approaching, and it allowed me time to make all the necessary arrangements. I would have the house to myself, without duty calling at every turn. However, that perk was short-lived. She was discharged a day before the city was buried under eighteen inches of snow, which would have been ideal conditions for writing, home alone.

The next day, the only sounds I heard were the snowplows trying to clear out the main arteries for emergency vehicles. With the pantry and fridge replenished and the heat keeping us warm, we settled into a mini-hibernation. I recall that when we were kids there were some economically challenging times. Eggs and rice with an occasional slice of spam or Vienna sausages were common dishes back then. As a result, I'd overcompensated to make up for the lack in the former tough times by stockpiling nonperishable canned goods and other long-lasting necessities. What I recalled most from the blizzard was the quiet, eerie feeling in its aftermath. In a few days walking paths were shoveled, and things got back to a semblance of normalcy before cabin fever had a chance to set in.

Trapped! A side effect of being housebound due to the storm was no escape from obligatory servitude. I was irritated. In an attempt to overcome the suffocating sensation, I marched myself to private caged quarters in my bedroom hammock in search of some liberating thoughts. Some of the moments that I recollected had been visited many times over, perfect get-away thoughts for catching my breath.

Fresh in my memory bank was my dad's sanctuary, a small dayroom at the front of our rented home in the Bronx. The apartment was decorated with bloated furniture covered with plastic. Gaudy lamps, homemade curtains, pictures of President Kennedy and the Last Supper, and too much memorabilia of other peoples' travels filled in the remaining niches. In contrast to the rest of our home, my dad's dayroom was a quaint retreat. The inventory surveyed in my recollection transported me. A row of windows framed the room's length and permitted unrestricted daylight. There was a hospital bed with a guard rail. A wall-to-wall closet had been built by a very close friend, Tony Zayas, who, after many years of comradeship, had been anointed family status for his generosity in building it. The room afforded enough space for my dad's canaries and his wheelchair. As a matter of routine, every other day he would sit in his wheelchair reading his newspapers, El Diario y La Prensa. Then he would close his door and open the bird cage portal. The clutter of canaries seeking restricted freedom clogged the entryway, like rush hour traffic.

Routinely, when I would come home from work, after Chuito and I exchanged some pleasantries, it was my welcome assignment to gather his feathery singing chorus for him. One by one I would gather them and escort them back to their confines. I felt like a jailhouse warden counting heads. Chuito was dedicated to his relationship with them. As a daily ritual, slices of orange and apples were wedged between thin wires. The water was boiled then cooled to a certain temperature, purified and changed regularly. Treats, bird seed, a mirrored bird bath, bells and assorted trinkets were carefully placed like furniture in their cramped living quarters. The gentle flutter of their wings tickled my palms as they struggled for their fleeting moments of freedom.

I always wondered if there was a trauma attached to their repeated capture. I suspected that my appearance in the room caused them concern and had them scattering to difficult niches. *Did they think ill of my presence; was I the bad boogeyman?* I looked at my dad; he was contemplative. *Did he view this room as his cage the way i currently saw my situation? Were his amputated legs, unable to exercise their freedom of movement, like clipped wings?* Usually, at the end of the tedious collection of uncooperative canaries, one last warrior still battled with defiant feathers for the right to take flight. As exhausted as it was, it submitted reluctantly to lockdown.

"What do you feel as they seek freedom? Once the cage door is opened, don't they have a choice between conditioning and self-rule?" I asked my father.

"A touch of envy," he replied. Smiling, he continued, "I'm jealous, yet their flight allows me to walk, dance and frolic. They are my legs, and it saddens me when they're caged. I know that pain all too well."

We learn, with time, the language of life's lessons. They are spoken with unforgettable authority; or articulated in silence. Moments can provide us a view of the horizon; or ambush us in dark alleys. I rolled him in his chair to the dining table and then scampered to my room for pen and paper (as I do now), thankful for the opportunity and the subject.

Those subdued days in my snowstorm-enforced retreat were a meditative marathon, for much-needed cleansing and uplifting. Peace and quiet had been robbed in Puerto Rico due to, for instance, the ice cream truck and the barking dogs. What a contrast! The avenues at night were free of ambulances and fire trucks. I doubt I could have paid folks to be out in these icy streets. The knuckleheads were indoors, so the cops had no one to beat up on. I was able to write without intrusions from anywhere, and that was wonderful. It was a Godsend.

Foforito had me all to herself. She kept busy with needlepoint, prayer books, and the TV. Given her hearing loss, she didn't seem to notice or mind when I muted the sound for even more peace and quiet. I sat at my desk and became mesmerized by the winter wonderland on the other side of the pane. The branches were coated with glittering ice; a relentless wind had the tree across the avenue dancing erratically. Streetlights gave the white peaks of snow piles prominence as the landscape had been transformed by the icy onslaught. A howl raised in my ear directed me back to my intention at the desk. I surveyed my room; the organized clutter dressed the inner landscape; trinkets and artifacts confirmed where I'd been and who I was, as one's digs well should. I felt at home, complete with a security blanket and warm slippers.

One evening Foforito beckoned. I stepped downstairs to her domain and was greeted with a grated-from-scratch cup of hot chocolate she had prepared and put on the table for me. The dim lights gave the dining nook a warm welcoming appearance. Her hair was unkempt, a flannel bata covered her from neck to ankle. She was blowing into the hot cup to cool her cocoa. The lids on her eyes were heavy, weather-beaten by time, yet there was an angelic look about her.

Foforito began to speak of disappointment and crowning achievements, her love for my dad, and missing those who had helped to enrich the quality of her life. There was a deliberate cadence in her tone. Her conversation warmed my heart as I sipped the hot chocolate from my cup. There was no talk of the inevitable, no dark view, no resentments, and no grudges or regrets. She was baring her soul, and I was her witness. A spontaneous shot of Mama Juana was added to the chocolate to further heat my innards as I lent an ear to her precious moments: unguarded, without fear, and raw with emotion. The room filled with an ember that continued to glow as the night wore on.

I sensed that Foforito had finally exhaled, and in reviewing her life's journey, she had become content with her present state. She had come full circle, from the mountain-scapes of Puerto Rico to our dining nook and had experienced resolution.

Playfully, I licked my palm and attempted to corral her unkempt thinning white mane. "Hey, get out of here," she admonished me, as her limbs fought off my silly gesture. I returned to my sanctuary and cried my sentiments into the pillowcase, which was becoming waterlogged during that poignant period.

The following morning, my downward climb had me shacking the cobwebs and straightening my bones Foforito was up and about; I could hear her monologue at a distance. It was a nonconfrontational tone, unlike most mornings when the ornery look and combative posture would be telling of my day's outlook.

"La Bendición," I yelled so she could catch my approach. Foforito's response resonated, "Que Dios te bendiga." Her blessing lifted the tension that sat on my shoulders like daily attire. Most of my precious moments with her were hatched over what I view as coffee break conversations. I bellowed, "¿Quieres café?" She laughed and responded, "¿Muerto quieres misa?" Cheese, crackers, and a hard-boiled egg accompanied the morning Joe. Somehow the verbal exchange shifted to questions we often entertained but seldom address. I asked her if there were anything that she would like to do in this life that until now has not been attainable. She paused, I could tell that she took the question seriously, rummaging her bucket list wants in the here and now. "I always wanted to drive." I thought for a moment; economics and culture had a hand in her not getting behind the wheel.

It was a brisk day; the sun coated my outlook with promise. Winter had withdrawn the leaves and deposited snowbanks; the day invited us to venture out. I didn't have to wrestle with her. She struggled into her bra and other accessories so she could leave the house. By all accounts, an adventurous moment was in the making. My girl was in a rare mood, so I decided to just drive. We finally ended up at Orchard Beach in the Bronx. The huge vacant parking lot invited me to provide her a moment behind the wheel. I stepped out the car, positioned her into the driver's seat. Her confused look didn't house any fear. This is the brake, and this is the gas pedal. She looked at me, "¡Tu esta loco!" With as straight a face as I could manage, I replied, "Hey, you wanna drive? Let's do it."

She convinced herself by mumbling that it felt like sewing... "sewing pedal, gas pedal, lo mismo." We did three loops around the parking lot without incident. She didn't exceed the five mile-an-hour speed limit, and the power steering helped her at the curves. I was relieved that it went smoothly, and she was elated that she drove. Thrilled to tears, she thanked me. In turn, I informed her that next week she could go for her license. The trip back home was filled with excited chatter. We even stopped to celebrate with a feast at City Island, a few miles away from her driving debut.

The next morning, I copied my driver's license, and pasted her picture on it. "You're official now!" We hugged, and Foforito secured her document. Upon reflection, I concluded she had always been in the driver's seat.

As the lingering snow was melting, Foforito's physical health and mental state were also undergoing serious changes. In the mornings, she was bitchy, unpredictable, condescending. Daily it had become necessary to rearrange my plans on a moment's notice according to her mood swings and the memory loss she exhibited on a more frequent basis. She repeated things constantly, so I began showing her family pictures to test her memory. We had an on-going dominoes tournament to help sharpen her focusing skills. The support of Medicaid paid, and out-of-pocket home attendants were a godsend. This provided windows of opportunity for me to navigate my own necessities. Their forty hours a week of service left me with one hundred and twenty-eight hours of duty, with no foreseeable change on the horizon. At times, the view was daunting.

My nightmares were more frequent and violent; I was constantly running away or in a confrontation. Foforito's unpredictability sabotaged my normal routines for her. Simply walking downstairs was no longer simple for her, and I had to be cautiously on guard. Out of the blue, she'd flip a switch. She was unsettled with a multi-personality; one of them was a trickster in an agitated huff. Medication to calm her down really wasn't an option, since I didn't want her to become a fall risk in a sedated state. Disaster on two flights of stairs would just be a matter of when. The thought of shoveling her off the hardwood floor didn't sit well with me. Foforito, generally, started to wilt by eight or nine in the evening. So, I commenced giving her responsibilities that I knew would whittle away at her energy; allowing me longer periods to exhale. It's funny how, saddled with cultural duty and with little recourse, I adjusted to the circumstances I had inherited.

She screamed. Springing from bed, I sprinted onto an area rug that skated under my feet, causing me to slip and land awkwardly on my back. A little dazed and bruised, I staggered to the landing and fumbled a painful and unsteady descent. The lights were out; her door was slightly open. The silence left me puzzled as I found my way to her bedside. She was sound asleep; dead to the world. I got close to her to make sure she was breathing. My presence startled her to attention.

"What are you doing?" she complained. I had invaded her peace, and it left her annoyed. She could not know how my peace of mind and body had been compromised, how her talking-in-her-sleep scream had infiltrated my downtime.

Returning to my bedroom, I glanced at a mirror parallel to my bed that captured a perplexed and troubled expression. As I settled back into bed, my body ached as the result of the fall and its painful aftermath. I was hurting physically, however, it was the emotional stress which I found most troubling.

Some hours later. I woke up sore and discombobulated. Foforito was awaiting my presence at her perch by the window. She had no recollection of the previous night's episode.

She: "What are we having for breakfast?"

Me: "I don't know, what are you making?"

Shuffling her way to the kitchen—once her domain—La Vieja took a 360-degree survey of the surroundings. "What would you like?" she asked. Then, answering her own request, she proceeded to rattle off a chef's list of her favorite recipes. "Let's start with some coffee," I countered, and then got her involved. Working with arthritic fingers, she forced a firm grip of the collador with one hand and poured the freshly brewed coffee with the other. The intoxicating aroma filled both our lungs. She then whipped the milk into foam. I boiled some eggs, sliced some cheese, toasted bread, and prepared a bowl of fruits. Belly full, Foforito whipped out a fresh list of complaints about one thing and the other. Sometimes it was best to just go with the flow.

I cleared the table and assigned her to dishwashing. She objected just as the home attendant arrived, so I reassigned the task. As Miriam began washing the dishes, Foforito wedged herself at the sink and wrestled with her, "I'll do the dishes." At times, I had felt that not having children was a blessing; maybe raising a parent had become the penance for not having done so. The scars of the missed opportunity to parent children of my own, like the ache of arthritis, visited me periodically as I tumbled with what could have been. The thought of me dealing with things like training wheels... me and missed curfews... me and chanclatazos... *Oh, boy!*

If I wasn't around, Foforito wasn't eating. She had taken to engaging in hunger strikes. It put a strain on the home attendants. I viewed it as her way of controlling and manipulating our relationship as well as a way to ease her insecurities.

The desk near the window provided me a haven for collecting my thoughts and spilling them on paper. As opportunity allowed, I maneuvered my way to what was a forbidden zone; since the flight of stairs to the third floor had become a bit too much for her those days. Subsequently, whenever she grew needy, she utilized the brass bell at the foot of the stairs, allegedly reserved there for emergencies. Although the snow had muted the street noise, she must have seen Quasimodo in *The Hunchback of Notre Dame* because the clanging became nerve-racking if I didn't appear to resolve one concern or another.

While sitting with my pen and pad, another snowstorm made its way to our neck of the woods. The flakes went from picturesque to turbulent to treacherous in a matter of moments. It simulated the course of events that had me in a quandary and buried my heart under an emotional avalanche. Circumstances had me simultaneously glaring out and looking within. The thought arose that every storm has its illustration, became a victim of the ensuing season, and was relegated to the natural order of things. That theory became a rallying cry moving forward. Whenever I found myself entertaining what was insignificant at day's end, taking those assessments to bed allowed me to be at peace with what was to come. *Funny, how the blizzard created the calm.* Revelations remain moot if we're not open to them. So, whenever a situation became muddled and the need for clarity was evident, I tried to pause in order to revive.

Ever since we had returned from Puerto Rico, unwelcome news had swirled like the storms, testing the strong and the weary. Soulo Zayas, a friend for over forty years, passed away from cancer. Although three others, including family members, also passed on to inevitability, Soulo's passing hit hardest. Years ago, whenever he would drop me off at the hospice where my brother Tony had died, Soulo would comment, "Leaving now." The connotation of that phrase varied, depending upon the circumstances. Those words resonated as I paid my respects and made my rounds. Similarly, my brother Al would always remark, "We know we're aging 'cause we spend more time at wakes and in hospitals than at parties and concerts."

Sitting at my desk, looking out at the void, I was grateful to be above ground, healthy, and tanned to boot. *Fuck whining.* This period was telling, and I was the recipient of good fortune, even if at times that thought was difficult to fathom.

On the morning of Foforito's 92nd birthday, my night's sleep must have been restless; pillows and a blanket in disarray on the bed and the floor were evidence that my altered state must have been very active. As I splashed water on my face, I could hear Foforito chattering downstairs. Entering her space, I saw she was in a delicate way; all her bedding was in a heap at the foot of the bed. She was nude except for a loose-fitting diaper. Ninety-two years of gravity pulling at her nipples, plus her shedding, unruly hair, and an ornery mask had her one wrinkled mess. Attempting modesty, she reached for the airplane blanket and wrapped it around like a shawl. *Too late, my dear, I already saw your boobs.* I chuckled, awkwardly. "They took everything, everything," she screamed. At the head of the bed, colored threads were scattered on the mattress like thin flower petals.

She'd been scratching dry skin; her irritated, leathery hide was sensitive, and a cruel reminder that age had imposed a mandated tax. She pulled her hair and bit her

145

hand in frustration. Luckily, the teeth were still in the bedside glass and the gum marks didn't break skin. I no longer became ruffled by those episodes, which I couldn't make up in my wildest dreams. I got her pajamas and a tee shirt, and dressed her wounds, chapped and brittle to the touch.

"I need my glasses," she demanded. After I deposited her night pail in the bathroom, removed her potty droppings and cleaned her pail; the attention pacified her. I shouted over my shoulder, "I'll call the detective." Then I headed downstairs to rustle up some grub. The farina and coffee were appropriate for that damp, dreary, snow-sloshing day. I brought her breakfast in bed. Grudgingly, she thanked me. "You're welcome, and good morning." She softened her tone and gave me her blessing, "Que Dios te bendiga."

After breakfast, I called up my brother to share that morning's episode. Maybe I could set up a dance pole and make some money here, I suggested sarcastically; or better yet, start a reality show for stripping seniors. Might as well be creative with the situation. He asked if I had a few singles to put in her sexy senior disposables for him, as we had a good-hearted laugh at Foforito's expense.

I looked over at her, oblivious to my conversation, "Al sends his love." She got mushy and told me to convey her blessings. Al had sent a package containing gifts, a card, and some pictures of the great-grandchildren. The gifts reflected the promise of spring, namely, the usual nylon socks that barely covered her ankles, and the cotton tee shirts that she always wore.

Anticipating Foforito's birthday, I had made plans to

drive down to Atlantic City with her so she could indulge her gambling addictions on a three hour trip. My friend, Tony, and his mother-in-law, Nana, accompanied us. Two hours before leaving, all her bras had mysteriously vanished, and her choppers were missing also. I located a bra in the shower; luckily, it was not wet. At a loss for where her teeth could be, something told me to look in the garbage can. Lo and behold! Her pearly dentures were wrapped in a paper towel along with Al's package! *I gotta checklist all her belongings prior to garbage day* was yet another task I added mentally to the to-do list. A few days later, another false teeth hunt was solved when I saw a napkin slightly stuffed into the soil of the plants by her sitting area in the dining room. Those escapades, bizarre and ill-minded, whittled away at my patience with an exactitude which percolated my attitude. Over time, the adventures were losing their humorous twist.

I was forgetting what spontaneous laughter sounded or felt like, and the healing rewards it presented. I tried to understand how tangled Foforito must have felt about her awareness being scrambled. I'd become convinced that her antics were in part a progression of the disease, and in part a way of controlling having her interests met. Her matriarchal position had worn out its welcome, and I wondered if she realized the divides created by her slicing criticism. My dulling armor became further tarnished by commentary. "I'm your mother," she muttered when I contested her pointed remarks.

Each day brought a new target. Today's rag doll was her sister Elsa, the youngest female of fifteen siblings. Elsa's home in Absecon, New Jersey was a pit stop as we headed to Atlantic City. Foforito resented those in the clan who had landed on cotton cushions and were educated to boot; they had been spared the unjust indignities that she, in her caretaking of them had inherited by default. That day she was erupting venom at unresolved issues which were always lurking, rearing their ugly heads at a moment's notice.

We were forced to stop at Elsa's home to relieve ourselves. Foforito was a mess and needed to be sanitized. After she corraled the muck, my Aunt Elsa was very accommodating as she tended to the damsel in distress. La Vieja softened her posture, while sipping some chamomile tea to soothe her tummy. Tony and Nana were a pleasant distraction from the tension my mother provided. By birth order, Elsa and my mother were the clan's bookend sisters. Usually, Foforito took umbrage even if unwarranted.

After our pit stop, Foforito picked up where she had left off, undoing Elsa's good intentions. Elsa was privileged, and she, Foforito, was the sacrificial lamb. As if being born into a more lenient place on the timeline as Elsa had been was a crime. I couldn't imagine my mother's youth. *Were her birthdays celebrated or considered gala worthy? Was she acknowledged, revered, given praise?* Unresolved issues reverberated, vandalizing her ability to move into the moment, obscuring her views of forgiveness. At day's end, peace of mind was an afterthought, and her anger was permanent and triumphant. Not a good mental place to celebrate one's day of birth.

Atlantic City was merciless. The one-armed bandits held up the birthday girl and relieved her of all her moola. In addition to being bitter, now she was broke. Around midnight, the trip back was made pleasant by Tony's company and the two mothers snoring in unison: music to my ears.

The next morning of the ongoing celebration of Foforito's ninety-second, I started preparing for well-wishers and family folk. The garden was transformed as welcoming niches were lit up with votives. The catered food got arranged, and an ice cream birthday cake was placed in the freezer. A congregation gathered who genuinely housed a fondness for Foforito. After all, she could be the most adorable, huggable doll in town when she was in her right mind. La Vieja became the center of attention, and it helped that those in attendance were folks she held in high esteem. Grandchildren, great-grandchildren, family, and friends joined in a chorus of love, which humbled her. The birthday girl blew out the candles and was first to benefit from the pastries and ice cream. She was lifted by the revelers and the tribute that placed her in the center of everyone's affection. The merriment took its toll as she withered into the night. When all the well-wishers had departed, I noticed my mother's purse had a bulge. I unzipped it to find a pouch stuffed full of pastries from yesterday's buffet at Atlantic City. I couldn't take the girl anywhere! Upstairs, Foforito crawled into bed where I covered her from head to toe. Without a doubt, a fitting way to end the birthday festivities.

Al called, but Foforito was sound asleep, so it allowed me a moment to vent. All he did was ask, "How you doing?" My response was lengthy and had some meat to it. I was frustrated, my options were limited, the support system had its restrictions, and I felt handcuffed. In these past few months, all the well-wishers were not volunteering frequently or consistently enough. I was isolated; my moments were no longer mine. I reminded Al how, in sacrificing for our family, Chuito had relinquished his aspirations for travel. Although ultimately his desire to visit Brazil was dashed after he became handicapped, it hadn't helped that Foforito always knew how to water down a dream.

I didn't blame her for our dad becoming handicapped. Nonetheless, she could muster a multitude of reasons not to do something we all should do, and that is to reward ourselves for being. One by one, dad's noble goals crushed under the squeaky sounds of a wheelchair seeking shade from the California sun.

Al interrupted, "Yeah, usually his decisions were his own, but she ambushed him with the, 'Ay bendito' bullshit. He gave in to her just to please her, and now she's doing it to you."

That statement arrested me. My mother had always played a role in the failure of my relationships. But at day's end, it had been I who had allowed her to wreak havoc. More than once I had even used her as an excuse to get out of a relationship; she had been my trump card. I'd been in denial all that time and was facing the consequences for those actions. If there's one thing I learned to appreciate from my brother, it was his honesty, even when it was brutal. I needed to find balance in my life... *really look within... investigate...* Through no fault of her own, my mother had emulated the person her mother had been. Apparently, by way of association, I mimicked some of those characteristics; three generations worth. Maybe I needed a ritualistic cleansing, or better yet, an exorcism. Could I learn how to shed those unwanted traits? In time, I gathered that the key was recognizing that they existed.

A walk by a playground allowed me to reflect on the concept of the seesaw as it revealed itself. The sitting points represented Ying and Yang; the center was the fulcrum. When there was movement there'd be a point where Ying and Yang saw eye to eye. That balance was a fleeting moment. Interestingly enough, it allowed me to view the action and its consequence, simultaneously. The answer sat in that counterweight.

On April 20th I went from celebrating my brother Tony's birthday to marinating bittersweet remembrances. The shady tree by the playground provided a beach-umbrella sanctuary as I reflected on Tony's short-lived life. My brother's passing was anticipated; he already had full-blown AIDS and was in a hospice. This loss had been sobering and left me staggered. After all those years, I still felt the void created by his absence. It seemed that those who had passed away got relegated to the past tense in the occasional communal or isolated conversations. That day I was engaging in the latter. I missed the link which once seemed so secure, wasted away by AIDS, the terrifying disease of our time.

Tony never got the opportunity to witness his daughter Ganya's graduation, even though it had been his efforts that provided her that opportunity. I admired the sacrifices he had made for his three cubs. In turn, Ganya rewarded her father's spirit with her professional accomplishments. Additionally, she and her brothers, Gibran and David actually mimicked their father's parenting skills and proceeded to raise his nine grandchildren, loving and responsible people, who live as Tony's legacy.

Tony, Foforito's middle child, was definitely her favorite. I believe this was from mutual entanglements that allowed her to exercise her maternal status. She spent many hours with him in emergency rooms, and over time, they had developed a special bond. As expected, Tony's illness and subsequent passing had crumbled Foforito. I had feared a downward spiral for her. Indeed, she grieved, but didn't allow grief to stop her. My girl managed her grief with occasional tears masking the sadness that surely lingered. Bravely, she went on living her life, while her nightly prayers always included my dad and my brother as permanent fixtures. Tony's death had morbidly reminded me that I was moving up on that death-row line, with no enthusiasm for my due date. Yes, my mother's calloused knees were buckled, but her resolve remained an example I needed to embrace.

The sound of the running brook at the Bronx River Parkway enlivened my moment. I had almost forgotten my original intent had been to visit brother-friend Tanco's mother, affectionately called Negre. On the day in question, she had been taken by ambulance for some exams, so I missed the opportunity to receive her blessings. It was interesting how our parents had become friends as a result of their children's bonding. Negre was a jovial soul, her well-rounded anatomy and puffy cheeks projected a regal presence, oozing with humility. The good tidings that always spilled from her lips somehow created a safety net for me and settled my rambunctious spirit. Sadly, she was saddled with mounting afflictions and had been confined to a bed for the last three years. Her braided white locks, cushioned by her pillow, were in sharp contrast to her buttery black skin, free of wrinkles. I recalled our last visit, sharing pleasantries that caused laughter to rise from her diaphragm and bellow into a room congested with medical supplies and adult diaper boxes. She had never recovered from her husband Bueyon's passing; a big chunk of her went with him. I missed also his imposing presence and the emerging smile that he would bestow on me whenever we met. As kids, we would always see him in his Kangol hat waiting for his beloved wife as she descended from the 41 bus.

Revisiting my past in the Butler Housing Projects, in the boogie down Bronx, I found myself in the place where most of my present friendships had been formed. The swing in the playground moved by a slight wind caused me to question why I was entertaining these thoughts. The view from the bench, the sandbox, the swings, and seesaw, along with the missed opportunity to see Negre, put things in context for me, allowed me to better understand the thoughts and emotions in which I had been engaging.

My brother had been the victim of racist ideology within our own family. Over many years there had been lines drawn in the sand around the issue of color. Our parents had played a role, either by ignorance or insecurity; neither of which were acceptable nor excusable behavior, in my opinion. So, it was a crippling betrayal for us to witness our parents' disapproving reaction when my brothers and I each choose a partner who was of a dark skinned complexion.

Ugly toxins of bigotry rose to the surface and caused me to distance myself from some people who were family by blood. Growing up, I had close relationships with Black kids, Latino or not. We ate together, shared toys. We had sleepovers at each other's homes. What about the Kelly family, Doña Regina, and dad's best friend, Frank? Bonded by circumstances established over time we had formed relationships that sometimes were more family than family. It had been the Tancos' generosity of spirit that prepared me to better embrace my African connection as a Puerto Rican. I owed them a debt of gratitude for their expressions of kindness focusing me to understand that any Puerto Rican, regardless of complexion, who didn't recognize his or her African roots was a Puerto Rican out of convenience.

And so, April 20th, Tony's birthday, conjured a delicate, dark time that still resonated. He had endured a difficult period in his life as a result of mindless affront. We three brothers had engaged and married women whose complexions were chocolate and caramel. Tony and his wife Eldona gave Foforito three loving Black Latino grandkids David, Ganya and Gibran. As the whispers and comments circulated, I divorced myself from some family members whose prejudices I considered noxious. Sitting on the bench, I still felt the sting of that intellectual deficiency, and the wedge that emanated from it. To her credit, Foforito eventually embraced the family that time had mandated. When she assimilated her new reality, she couldn't feed those kids enough alcapurrias, food being her personal signature of love and family. I'd come to realize that my mother, even with her fears and apprehensions, was an incredibly adaptable person. In spite of having little to no formal education, Foforito had risen to a point of contentment, because she recognized her errors in judgment and the pain they had caused.

Parenthetically, that is not to say, as some might, that having a formal education includes having moral instruction; in fact, I believe the reverse is more accurate. Foforito's change of heart was just that; her lack of formal schooling wasn't in the mix. It had been her own heart. Ultimately, it was the unresolved issues with her mother that had crippled my Foforito's ability to travel light and be at peace with herself. Grudges could silence one's spirit, while learning and exercising forgiveness can set one free. I continued to struggle with that simple piece of wisdom.

The police officer was quite civil when he informed me that, without a child, I wasn't allowed in the playground. I was just idling with my pen, and the park was vacant except for my thoughts. I gathered my belongings without questioning the rule and didn't personalize that moment, since sometimes it's best to leave it alone. I headed crosstown to the Cloisters, feeling a need to separate myself from mundane routines. It helped that Miriam was at the house and flexible if I were late. Like a truant, I felt I was escaping duty to obligations. I nested by one of the many garden niches and scribbled until my fingers cramped.

Foforito had always enjoyed this sanctuary; however, that day it was a solo flight. I called Miriam to let her know I was running late without going into detail. She told me to be at ease with myself, "I'll see you when you get here. Besides my son knows how to make a sandwich for himself." I compensated Miriam for her time and also drove her home. When I returned Foforito was napping. Later that evening Foforito was entertained by a Yankee baseball game and delighted with a bowl of vanilla ice cream before both of us called it a day.

———◆———

Breakfast was a perfect meal: a grilled cheese sandwich—not too toasted, lightly buttered; a hardboiled egg—not too soft, not too hard, little salt, sprinkled pepper; regular coffee—not too light, because then it's not coffee, it's tainted milk. The coffee was not too dark, because that's better for her Mercedes Benz engine.

Carefully, on the far side of the bed I placed the tray full of good intentions, including the classy touch of a freshly picked rose. Foforito was fast asleep, curled up in fetal position. I awakened her by rubbing her shoulder, brittle to the touch. If startled, she gets pissed off and sets the tone for her day. She stuck her head out from the comforter like a turtle. With her scalp sweating through her unkempt hair from the layers of bed covers, my moms looked like a cross between a punk rocker and a wet chicken. Peeling off the layers reluctantly, she gave me that "I'm not a morning person" look.

She inspected the tray and said, "Wow!" Then, in the same breath, complained the room was cold and proceeded to sit on the pail that was her potty, which gave her a jolt because it was cold also. It provided me a moment of laughter. Foforito, in turn started giggling, then her flailing hands dismissed me for a moment of privacy. I handed her a wash towel, which she flung back to me once her hands were sanitized.

Then, she dug into the well-intended grub. I pictured the tray with its contents, as a hat atop her head. Erasing that thought, I made my way downstairs. The ritual became my morning chant; it resonates in the garden of my remembrances. That was only breakfast... there was still the rest of the day to be had.

Mom and me... Her sense of entitlement had reached a stage vacant of appreciation. Not that I was seeking any kind of gratitude from her. No, what twisted my nerves wasn't the lack of recognition. It was the demeaning accusations and depraved indifference that deflated my best intentions. Harsh words, yet they portrayed an accurate account of the handful she'd become.

Sometimes, to evaporate the anxieties of being a caretaker, I escaped to the gazebo nestled in the backyard. There, handmade waterfalls cascaded from positioned pots, gourds, and pieces of bamboo and landed into a makeshift pool. Thriving water plants with names I couldn't pronounce grew abundantly. The pump at the base, carefully camouflaged by ferns, circulated water back up the plastic tubes. Wearing her pink polyester pants, Foforito had joined me, ready to prune and earn her keep. I gave her a broom and let her exercise. A stickler for detail, she worked the broom into niches filled with neglect. Slowing down, the lady who had always been hands on, was only able to perform in spurts. In the name of good cardiovascular exercise, I allowed her to do whatever she could.

On the other side of the gate by the gazebo, some young brothers were just hanging on one corner. Another corner had Jehovah's Witnesses promoting their beliefs. One promised salvation; the other flirted with incarceration. I navigated my way to the local bodega for my newspaper. Rugged winds the night before had separated leaves and disturbed budding clematis flowers before their maturity. The dead foliage had been escorted by Foforito's broom out of all the nooks in the garden and created small piles which she later placed into the trash one pile at a time. Foforito had been relentless with her sweeping and pruning task. Prying her away, I sat her down to catch her breath, as her panting had become noticeable. I collected the rest future compost and deposited it in the garden bed.

Last night's storm had brought to light how delicate life can be. It also illustrated the seasonal changes and how they compare to personal cycles. As gardeners of our lives, we nurture, feed and communicate, we attract butterflies; birds chirp their songs of gratitude, bumblebees collect nectar; it's a natural cycle. My mother, in her winter, clung to branches in search of the memories that had escaped her, as she prepared for her inevitable ending.

Just when I thought I had no more tears to shed, I found a few I needed to share. La Vieja was sitting in the nook, honed by time to fit her frame. She appeared to be fine-tuning the art of being well-liked. Recently she seemed to have been trying to develop a character not prone to complaining so much and appreciative for things given to her. As if witnessing her own transformation, she became fixed with a wayward look. *What could possibly be churning inside?* Memory could be a cruel trickster; it opened windows to view the moments that defined former periods of fulfillment. Then, in an instant the heart is hung naked, flapping in aloneness.

Her searching gaze seemed to be unsuccessfully attempting to link one thought to another. Caught in the dark corners of a labyrinth, her remembrance became corralled and twisted, with each turn presenting fragmented images of the past. Two huge shadows gathered beneath reddened eyes. The dark bags they formed were filled with sentiment. I mustered the will to reel her back and asked her what she was thinking. As she turned her face into full view, I read a paragraph of unanswered thoughts across her forehead. She replied simply, "Your father." I approached her from the rear, wrapped my arms around her frail frame and whispered, "I miss him too." I understood the tears wetting her wrinkles as I blew my own sentiments into a handkerchief.

Craving a refill, I prepared another batch of coffee and strained it through the colador. The intoxicating scent of freshly brewed Bustelo filled my nostrils. With a proud posture, I investigated the garden's progress, as I headed to my designated pigeonhole under the gazebo. I observed a neighbor making a mad dash to the bus, which started to pull away as he neared the door. He went off on the driver with a mouthful of profanities. I yelled out, "Hey, want some coffee?"

"Fuck you," He spouted out due to his lost day, before he realized it was I who was yanking his chain.

"Have a good one," I responded, as I took another sip. *People are always in a hurry to go to places they don't want to be.* To think, I was there once and had survived that conditioned madness allowed me the privilege of enjoying my garden and its evolving beauty. The day had gifted me a better appreciation for the healing I could attain while tending to my garden. It had become a sanctuary, rewarding my spirit with moments of reflection. I went back inside for a few moments to put on a repeat Yankee game for Foforito. The TV was her babysitter. Since she had been cooperative, I prepared her an egg cream, with a scoop of vanilla ice cream. Sipping it with satisfaction, she was in her element. Down in the garden, I lit votive candles and placed them strategically next to the Buddhist stone figures that stood guard, although camouflaged by bushes and vines. The colorful plants provided an air of calm as I recited, to the audience of myself, poems which I'd memorized over time.

A light breeze ruffled leaves that vibrated an energy alongside the rhythmic social discourse of passionate poetry. Serenity stood guard at the entryway, intent on shielding me from the ills on the other side. Casually, I started soaking the plants to their delight, as their fragrances filled the night.

A shadow appeared at the entryway from the kitchen. It was Foforito beckoning, "¿Que haces?" I put out my evening cigarette and let her know I'd be in soon. She stood her ground until I made my way inside. There were lucid moments in which I could entertain her in grounded conversation. Whenever that occurred, I used them to record meaningful events in her life.

"I didn't like your father at first," she started.

"Why not?"

"He had an air about him."

She had seen him as a player in a sweatshop full of women who were the recipients of his perfumed compliments. I poured some coffee and coaxed her, squeezing information that was real, heartfelt, and tender. Her story continued. One day she had attempted to open a window to allow in fresh air; they didn't call them sweatshops for nothing. The weight of the window and the weak chain that held it became a guillotine that smashed her finger. Chuito offered to take her to the hospital, and as a gentleman, stayed with her until they addressed her injuries. Then he escorted her home. That was the beginning of a courtship that lasted until my dad passed. For several hours, Foforito and I shared a gabfest filled with tasty tidbits of information that could only be found in our exclusive banquet.

The ensuing months were a potpourri of my mother's both lucid and abstract comportments. She would be in the moment, and then a flip of the switch had her searching for lost thoughts. It saddened me to view the transformation up close. My girl was starting to lose it, and I was bearing witness to that demise. The doctors were back to suggesting prescriptions to sedate her. Still, seeing her in a drugged, catatonic state wasn't an option that I could have lived with.

In addition, my health issues surfaced. First it was sciatica, which clung to me with a mean vengeance. Acupuncture and other holistic methods were only temporary relief valves. Then the nightmares started to trespass. I would awaken from acting out the end of each one. A rare night out found me in Gloria's (who I was seeing at the time) bed. Like a jack-in-the-box, I sprang from the four-poster, pressed the rewind button, and pounced back into the sack. Subsequent episodes became increasingly more bizarre.

In one nightmare, alone in my bed, I found myself arguing with a sanitation crew for not picking up my trash. In the skirmish, the garbage truck started barreling down on me. Taking off like a track star, I sprinted out of bed into the marble fireplace, which didn't budge. Although fearful of the damage to my head and face, I started assessing the vandalism to my collectibles. Sitting on the edge of the bed, I tried to get a grasp of what had just taken place. The alarm clock with its illuminating light was posting 3:30 in the morning! *Shit, what the fuck is going on?*

With a birdbath splash and a reluctant look in the mirror, I tried to put my finger on the pulse of the obvious. A few things were going on: a view of past mistreatment, irreversible abuses, and the trampled reality of Foforito's descent into dementia. The one-two punch left me on wobbly knees. A sizable scrape along my thinning hairline surrendered a chunk of hair; as well, a canary-egg lump was cause for concern. *This is some serious damage.*

I remained on the bed, feeling rattled and uncomfortable in my aloneness. Clutching my pillow, I continued to think about the premonitions that, figuratively and literally, had been waking me from my vulnerable sleep. A half-hearted chuckle emanated from images of myself in head gear or worse yet, placing a fence around the bed. Trying to make light of a dark situation and the irony that accompanied it had its moment, until I refocused on the noticeable physical damage. What concerned me most was the condition of my internal wiring.

Innermost upheaval and subliminal messages were giving my analytical mind a run for the money. The common theme in the dreams was running away. These trying times, this prolonged tour of duty was pulverizing my good intentions. I heard a clatter that needed attention before it escalated into chaos. Foforito's rosary beads had grown legs. The hunt for misplaced rosary beads cut into breakfast preparations.

"Gotta call the detective again," I blurted; my resolve was waning along with my patience. She gave me that, "Don't fuck with me and find my beads" look. Then she ran off the lineage of the beads. "They belonged to my mother, she gave them to Teresa, Teresa gave them to Alberto, Alberto gave them to me."

My mother could have been a writer; her stories unfolded like fine fabric that she was trimming with lace. "What are they going to think?" Being in an accusatory and antsy state did not serve her; it only promoted anxiety as she struggled to return upstairs. Such frenzy had her gasping, so she sat on the steps to gather herself. Dramatically, the heaving intensified until she stumbled into bed like a wounded cowboy in a spaghetti western. As the bed received her with delicacy, the rosary beads slid from beneath the pillow. I scooped them up and presented them to her. Miraculously, the heaving stopped.

She: "Oh, thank you, God!"

Me: "SHIT! Don't I get any credit here?"

She started up anew. "These aren't my rosary beads, they..." Her voice faded as I exited, unwilling to entertain the history lesson and tantrum at hand. "Why do you do this to me?" Her voice pierced through the air from upstairs as I started to prepare breakfast.

Having built up an appetite from her previous outbursts, she shoveled the grub down, then asked for a glass of water. I accommodated her request and positioned myself to the other side of the French pocket doors, which served as a buffer between her living quarters and the recreational room. I watched her. The panes partially insulated the wailing about rosary beads she had resumed on the other side of the glass.

New rules. I established a designated place for Foforito's personal belongings Everything would be safe, sound and easy to find. The mandate was that all precious items would be placed there. A nightly inventory check was added to my to-do list. The hope was to keep the detective at bay.

With a full day of duty before me, I started my domestic chores. The morning's episode had worn on Foforito and she napped, purring like a kitten. Surfing the boob tube, I came across a Carole King and James Taylor concert. I took a break to place calls to a few friends who would appreciate the show. Just about all the conversations turned to caretaking and the duties that consumed our daily calendars. Hearing that so many of my contemporaries were, in varying degrees, living similar circumstances was a sobering discovery. It was a sweet and sour moment: nice to know I wasn't alone in my struggles; saddened that our lives had been derailed by duty.

My chores took a backseat to this nostalgic event. Instead I sang along in my head the familiar words: *"I've seen fire and I've seen rain...", "so far away...", "you've got a friend..."* But then, hungry, needy and nasty, my

Sleeping Beauty awakened demanding attention. I asked if she would like to watch a movie, maybe *Throw Momma from the Train* would be a good choice.

Finally, we settled down and managed to salvage sanity by watching old movies and snacking. As time passed I thought about the needs of elderly folks in general, and Foforito in particular. There were many things, but perhaps the most important was a little attention and plenty of love; simple ingredients I could provide one day at a time.

Before I tucked my girl in, I took all her personal belongings and placed them in the Foforito Safe. Glasses, needlepoint, threads, rosary beads, and other diverse articles; the prayer books were placed in her personal niche. Since it was garbage pick-up night, I had to secure her false teeth, as well. Foforito was wilted from a lengthy day. My to-do list was completed.

With a comforting glass of white wine and an evening smoke, I retreated to the alcove by the gazebo. As a fog settled in, the streetlights glistened; the view was misty. A bus sputtered to a stop, and regular folks headed to their own realities. Those muted moments were periodically assaulted by boom boxes in passing cars, highlighting the indifference by those seeking attention.

In time, a calm settled in, and a sadness consumed me. The task at hand brought questions that weren't easily answered. I'd spent a good part of my life alone, selfish with my ways, and always asserting my independence. Knowing that there are consequences we must bear for the choices we make, I questioned: *Who will care for me? Will I land in a heap? Will I be discarded as irrelevant?* The sounds of sirens startled me to attention. I captured the salty liquid secreted on my cheek, almost unaware that I had allowed it to escape.

Each stage of the Foforito's journey towards inevitability presented specific behaviors. I began observing some of her antics. I particularly noted how the abusive episodes of her past had damaged her and shaped the personality she had become. I remembered when I came home one day, she was so excited. "I cooked for you." When I went to the oven: nothing. She immediately blamed Aida. "That woman ate everything!" My mother never assumed responsibility for anything gone awry or for the things she imagined.

I understood. The verbal and physical assaults she had endured as an abused child had forced her to develop a defense system that pointed fingers or completely threw folks under the bus. She had been beaten for, "not clean enough...", "not fast enough...", "not perfect." It appeared she was predestined to accuse and punish even the innocent in order to be perfect; and to save herself. Viewing those traits and understanding that I could inherit and mimic some of these self-serving attributes had me mindful of the work I needed to do to shed some baggage. Also, I reminded myself never to rob a bank with her.

One Saturday morning, neither my mother nor Aida wanted any part of the beach that day, so I did a solo. Day trips with the two of them to the Cloisters, various botanical gardens, and the zoos had become commonplace. Secretly I was thankful that they chose to stay behind, as I escorted myself from Jersey City to the Rockaways in Queens, New York and spread my blanket on the sand at Riis Beach. The unrestricted air filled my lungs. Duty-free, I savored moments so rare at that time. The thought of not being responsible for another person's happiness was refreshing. I felt my spirit recharge; I embraced carefree. The waves clashed with beach chatter. A persistent breeze threatened umbrellas as a migration of sun-worshipers invaded the plots of sand still available. Two Hershey-colored girls, no more than five and six years old, migrated in a pogo-stick-styled hop to the ocean's edge. Like ballerinas suspended on their tippy toes, they teased the waves. Their neatly braided hair sparkled with enthusiastic fervor as uninhibited laughter filled the air.

Two o'clock neared, announcing time for my departure. But not before I took a dip, even though the shoreline had a dingy appearance and was littered with foreign objects. Content with the joy of my morning and early afternoon, I scuttled past the parade of those folks who remained and packed up for the drive to my unknown. As I headed to the car, on a call from one of my caretaking contemporaries, Rudy announced his father's passing. And so, there would be another wake on the calendar to remind me of the inevitable.

In the car I chose to celebrate Rudy's dad's passing by playing some island music I thought he would have enjoyed. What a day! Shortly after Rudy hung up, Pete called from Puerto Rico to announce that his dad had also crossed the big divide. It seems that after an avalanche of illnesses culminating with amputation, Pete father's downward spiral had been rapid. Water-filled lungs, a heart attack, a stroke: like a semi-automatic gun, pow, pow, pow! The silver lining, if one could determine that losing one's parent has a silver lining, was that, in the end his suffering had been swift. Empathizing with my long-distance brother-friend, I was realizing that some of our elders know when it is time to let go of the maladies that twisted their living into suffering. Others held fast to the final ethers, either by instinct or fear. Curtis Mayfield was so on point when he sang, "Everybody wants to go to heaven, but nobody wants to die."

Upon my arrival home, I began writing letters of condolences. As was custom, I lit candles, symbolic of clarity which should be part of everyone's passing. My mom had been in relatively good health, with no urinary tract infections or other physical shortfalls. Her tantrums, unruly commentaries, and bizarre outbursts were like the stock market, up and down; erratic. I tried to stay away from the thought of Foforito's passing. But it was reality and having things in order was so important. I was caretaker and designated proxy. That thought, combined with the deaths of my two friends' parents, caused me to reevaluate those issues with a sense of urgency. What a day, that day.

The evening landed with oppressive heat, void of a breeze. The sway of my dayroom hammock in that invasive heat pulled on my eyelids until I surrendered. A dream clinging to me like the humidity was an unwelcome guest overstaying its visit. In the dream, Foforito was bedridden, a shell of herself, too frail to fight on. Holding her lifeless hand, I wondered about her persistent moans and what was happening inside of her.

Was she saying final wishes or speaking her discomfort?

Was she reciting her rosary?... mumbling goodbye?

———◆———

Even as we held hands in that dream state, I sensed our
contact thinning.

Is she peaceful?

*Will Chuito take her hand, lead her from darkness to
light?*

Will he be dancing as promised?

———◆———

Unsettling thoughts. I tried to read her blank stare. My
cynical views clashed with her Pearly Gate ideology. *Is
there a Supreme Maker, supreme make-believe? Will
her faith reward her? Is all of it a charade? A cruel joke?*
Despite my contradictions, I prayed for her; tried to take the
leap. I hoped her devotion would accompany her to where
I couldn't travel with my sarcastic, untrusting views of the
everlasting. My dream-self wrestled and wished that her
prayers and pains would be answered soundly. *Whoever
is listening, may she attain peace?*

As my dream continued a labored pulse beat in Foforito's
disjointed wrists. The pronounced veins of her hands and
tiny, tough-cut nails—never manicured or painted—were
evidence of her toil with nature. Being mandated to aid her
on her passage had me reluctantly questioning my own
place in time. Dream or no dream, my mortality remained
open for debate and was shelved for future review.

I swayed in my hammock cocoon, unable to exit. A
sudden thunderstorm became insistent, smacking the
panes and finding its way past the blinds onto the wooden

floorboards. I was a slingshot from the hammock into my slippers. My hurried steps found me huffing by her bedside. I hesitated, unsure, still dangling between my dream and my reality. I touched her lightly. Startled, she mumbled, "You want to scare me to death?" With exhilaration and frustration, I replied, "No, I just wanted to make sure you were alive." Then I returned to my bed, frazzled from dream demands and doings. All signs pointed to, TIME TO WRITE.

———————

At the time, I was dating a well-intentioned, hard-working woman who was a single parent and caring for her mother. Regrettably, this relationship developed out of the fear which consumed my periods of aloneness, rather than from the zing of a heartfelt connection. In retrospect, we were consoling each other's compromised plights; unfortunately, ties of romance were side-swiped and never came to fruition. Foforito's jealousy was a venom I was unable to manage while trying to develop a significant relationship. Ironically both women had a similar past laced with struggle. Nonetheless, I was beginning to see my mother in a different light, and it wasn't pretty.

In any event, as always, there was a reverence for the trajectory; and a sadness when it was over. At times, I felt as if I'd wasted all the opportunities that life had presented me in terms of interpersonal relationships. All the women in my life, starting with my grandmother Eugenia, had been nurturing. Perhaps losing her at such a tender stage of my emotional life caused me to be overtly guarded with my feelings. That separation had made its impact on me early on. I often felt she had taken my developing sentiments with her when she died.

Was I blessed or cursed in the province of romance? Those who placed affection on my shoulders at some point in the relationship were cast aside, along with the fondness that each provided. The lone reward had been that I'd hoarded the gifts of warmth and utilized them as comforter when I embraced reflection.

The light of day fought its way past the wooden blinds. I cursed the ineffective filters for not guarding my dreams to an uninterrupted conclusion. The illuminating rays challenged me to rise and appreciate another day above ground. Stretching, I separated my potential from my insolence. Sunday was 'Me and Mama Day', and it requested our presence. So, I cleared the path for this priority.

Foforito was positioned in her usual spot admiring a new batch of pink roses that matched her pink polyester pants. "La bendición," startled her to attention. Yet, "Que Dios te bendiga," resonated. After breakfast, she began complaining that a water bottle had fallen on her toe. I massaged her back until she panted. Then I whispered in her ear, "Let's take a ride." She pointed to the toe. I countered, "What about the other nine, why should they suffer?" She found that statement humorous and submitted. The ride to Bear Mountain was picturesque, and she was feeling it. She was a real trooper as we made our way to the picnic grounds. The date on the newspaper alerted me, it was August 26th, the anniversary of my father's death. I shared that with her. She reached into her vest pocket for her rosary beads and delivered her invocation.

It had been twenty-eight years since his passing, and it was the first time that I had been derelict in duty. I recollected that Junior, (my brother from another mother), had called, and he told me, "Dad died today." The jolt was piercing yet anticipated. I had hung up the phone, taken out a bottle of liquor, and started spinning his music. In making plans for the funeral and all the paperwork, I became consumed with duty. It haunted me that I didn't permit myself a moment to share with him my tears of gratitude. He had saved my life with the wisdom in his storytelling, but more important by his example. When I last saw him, he was a double amputee diabetic, suffering with a heart condition, and nearly blind. I was relieved he no longer would see himself as a burden and was free of the tribulations that had become permanent staples. And yet, it churned in me that I had not been able to squeeze a tear for this charismatic personality who had always been present in my life. This date also marked the twenty-eighth anniversary of the day my brother Al and I began the joint custody of our mother.

As the sun started to lose its luster, Foforito and I decided to grab a leisurely bite. The landscape was fertile, and the attention we received allowed us a moment to reflect. Our larger-than-life figure had given us the gift of a lifetime of his commitment as steward to his wife and offspring. Dinner, dessert, and the ride back home paid homage to him, as stories of remembrance were served back and forth. If Chuito had been eavesdropping, he surely would have been tired of all the accolades. Even though he merited every single one, sugar-coated or not. Foforito landed like a sack of potatoes after she gave me a big,

172

mushy hug. I schlepped my way into the shadows of my dimly lit room and stripped naked. In my quiet moment of stillness, I recollected Chuito.

I remember I had been eager to provide my parents with their own personal space, I quickly converted Al's garage into a home for them. I knew my dad didn't want to be there but pleasing his wife was the only thing he could afford to give her at that juncture. He would sit under the shady tree at the end of the walkway, rosary beads handcuffing his enormous hands. Apparently Chuito welcomed my chatty intrusions during these obligatory moments of devotion. He shared that his station in life was his to own and accepted the consequences of his present state. He understood that the disease was consuming him. A patch over one eye allowed him to have a better view out the other, and that was a blur. He had adjusted to losing his legs, but the loss of vision he struggled with was cruel and unjust penance. We joked about matters of consequence, laughed from the belly and discovered a mutual respect that remained full of fervor.

Chuito had shared a story, serious in tone, of a man who had it all: A wonderful mate, two loving children, his professional status unblemished, and a welcoming home. That picture was shattered by an accident in which his arm was amputated. Despondently walking along a road, he saw a truck and contemplated suicide. Before he acted, he saw a man on the opposite side with no arms dancing. He ran to him and thanked him for saving his life. "Here I am with one arm and I want to kill myself. "You have no arms and you're dancing!" The man responded, "I'm not dancing, my ass itches and I can't scratch it!" I was at peace in that moment, knowing Chuito's afflictions had not destroyed his humor, wit, and perhaps more importantly, his wisdom.

On that last day, the fog sat like a cloud of impending doom. My belongings were packed and stationed by the door. I sanded my heels against the pavement and placed my hands in my dad's. They felt defeated, and it crushed me. He resumed his posture; as we hugged, a mutual meltdown allowed our sentiments to meld. Those moments reverberated and were still tinged with teardrops. After all these years, I felt privileged that he had deemed me worthy of expressing our sentiments at such an intimate moment. In revisiting that interlude, I could finally reconcile my absence of tears during the time when he passed. I had deposited them already at the foot of his wheelchair when we hugged under the tree; not one more was left to shed. My sister-in-law Rosie, (Al's former wife), had held Chuito's hand in his last moments. She shared with us that my father's final words before he slipped away were, "Get me my shoes, I'm going dancing tonight." How appropriate. Time teaches us the importance of resolving issues and coming to terms; how to complete the circle and be at peace with those who really love you.

Foforito and I rose the next morning still stimulated by the previous day's recollections. Both of us sure that some of the revisions were enhanced and others were just painful reenactments of sentiments that had become obscured over time. I guessed as we had placed one foot and then another, we had lost sight of that which wasn't documented or maybe the starting points of those adventures. There was a beauty in storytelling as we retained our inquisitive natures. Foforito appeared a little discombobulated, as had become her pattern in the morning hours. Time was eroding the roots that once grounded her. I began to view that down-tempo skid gathering momentum like a mudslide in slow motion. Foforito's unsteadiness caused her to cling to the walls, tables, and other furnishings to steady her balance. Once she felt firm on her legs, she made her descent to the kitchen. Even when unsure and on rickety legs, she refused to accept assistance. I feared her hearing loss was affecting her equilibrium. That day, she moved about as if caught in a storm. The step up to the dining platform was challenging. Her recent dizzy spell and wobbly legs placed me on high alert.

"Oh, my God," she spurted, "Help me, God." Rosary beads in hand, her devotion leaped to attention, and it rejuvenated her. I suggested that we go upstairs so she could lie down and relax. She burped a grunt, rose reluctantly, and proclaimed, "Getting old sucks."

Her view from the landing presented the unwelcomed obstacle; again, she placed a call to God, as if she had a direct line to him. The line must have been busy, so I substituted in his apparent absence. Every other step was a resting station. She sat, tapped, and with droopy eyes looking right into mine, she expressed exasperation, "Me canso viendo el agua correr." The comment provided us a lighthearted moment in the darkness of the stairwell's cove. At the top of the landing she exhaled, triumphantly. Foforito's mounting collection of imperfect lines scratching her appearance were telling. I had known the smooth textured skin, fancy hairdos, and spunky disposition. I had been fascinated by her amusing wit and focused foresight.

In my mind, aging could be beautiful wrinkles; and aging could really suck.

After her extended nap, she asked me if I wanted some oatmeal, I let her know she had slept all day and it was evening. Moments later, she asked again if I wanted some oatmeal.

"It's dinner time," I tried not to roll my eyes in frustration.

"I'm a hundred years old, what do you expect?"

A miraculous leap from ninety-two to a hundred. It was a goal I think she would have liked to attain. It must be crushing to witness the decline of one's health as it becomes a permanent partner with the decay of one's memory. *One day, will I have to search for misplaced thoughts? Am I strong enough for that?* I wrote at times, because it liberated me. I wrote in as much as it defined me. I wrote because it explained away the ills that consumed me. I wrote more so to never forget the journey with its humorous twists. I reflected about the strength of the human spirit.

Lower back pain had arrived with plenty of luggage and without a date of departure. An appointment with my acupuncturist, Luis Hernandez, provided temporary relief, as I tried to juggle handling my afflictions with Foforito's. The daily stress of caretaking chiseled away at my resolve. Whenever I thought the dam was secured, another leak caused me to realign my view. A series of emergency room visits with Foforito landed her at Christ Hospital. By way of repair, within two years, labored breathing, heart palpitations, urinary tract infections and a procedure to correct rectal muscle failure were addressed. Subsequently, those visits and stays became commonplace. Each episode dwindled her outlook and sent her into prolonged periods of rehab.

What motivated me to stay the course was her desire to stand erect and move forward like a true warrior. I rewarded her efforts and remained present. The hospital and the rehab staff knew that *this* vieja had an advocate who was on duty 'round the clock. That made for smooth transitions back to the house. I remained humble and full of gratitude for the attendants who aided in those recoveries. I reflected on how Aida and Miriam had taken one hand each, my left and my right, and ushered me over hurdle after hurdle. They and I had formed a bond which helped me navigate the unpredictable waters of elder care for the two-plus years that we three would share.

<hr />

The mystery of dementia caused me to recall a previous trip to Puerto Rico. While there, I had visited Cotín, my father-in-law, perhaps one of the most interesting folks I'd ever met. He had become saddled with dementia and was in the advanced stages of the disease. A date for dinner found him a little tattered; the dented persona, so unlike the manicured regal posture that had been his staple. I was alarmed by his present state. Bathing had become a rarity at that time. I was concerned about his hygiene and wrinkled appearance; but not embarrassed. This once worldly figure, scented with Old Spice and seasoned by all his travels as a merchant marine, was frail and unkempt. I felt saddened that this robust chiseled body with the GQ air was but a shadow on the dark side of his traveled road. I spruced him up, and decided to take him to an upscale restaurant, Aquaviva.

The click-clack clatter of our shoes on the blue adoquines of Old San Juan announced our mutual hunger pangs. I understood there had to be a story about his recent circumstances, but what I wanted to entertain was his past. Cotín was a fascinating storyteller who relished a platform for weaving his tales; and he relived them with seasoned emotion. I asked about his most enjoyable dining experiences. He allowed me a safe passage to all his stamped ports of entry. I kept peppering him with a profound interest of his journey from its youth to the adult life at sea. The waiter brought assorted clams imported from different locales, seasoned with radish, lemon juice, and a sweet and spicy red sauce. Shells piled up and another order was placed. Cotín gently twirled the stemmed glass of wine between his fingers. His discourse included respected comrades, anchorage points, and of course, women; an old sea dog to the bitter end. Spain, Brussels, Amsterdam, India, and various cities within the continent of Africa, to say nothing of his trips to Central and South America, were among the countless global places Cotín revisited as he wet his lips with the wine of remembrance.

Cotín punctuated those significant adventures and unforgettable experiences with beaming eyes and fueled lungs. I felt honored and tickled that he had this transformational moment on my watch. The waitress asked the disheveled world traveler if everything was okay. He looked at her adoringly and bellowed, "I feel like a king!"

Those sitting nearby raised their glasses of wine. Although void of his once youthful physique, his lungs expanded with pride and filled his ribcage to capacity. He continued to butter up the waitress in the same fashion he used to address his warm bread, which would become worthy of sponging up the gravy of a meal suitable to his escapades. Flattery was a tool he had perfected to disguise his rough edges. As the blushing waitress exited, he turned to me with a devilish look and asked, "Now, where was I?"

His hearty laughter filled the place with his presence. That evening was cast in stone for me; I washed down dinner with espresso and a shot of anisette.

The ride back was sobering. Time had turned a former flawless trophy into a shattered souvenir. I felt like the driver of Cinderella's pumpkin coach. The slippers he slid into were all too real, not silver-lined with the "he lived happily ever after" ending. All those Old Spice stories were shelved, ready to gather dust again.

He gifted me two gallons of coconut water and as usual reverted to his catalogue of insults. "Take care of yourself, you fuckin' bum." Considering the source, I really didn't mind the well-intended slander. It was Cotín's way of telling me he loved me. That episode also made me aware of the importance of extracting the valuable heartbeats of my past as opposed to trying to make sense of the present. Sometimes our past cushions our descent and allows us to savor the good fortune in our journey. Sometimes our past crashes down on our good intentions and sabotages whatever lurks around the bend.

As with Cotín, entertaining Foforito in her world allowed me more access than trying to reel her into mine. Watching her from a seat opposite hers at our dining table, Foforito's intense gaze caused me to wonder. In the past quarter century, the journey had had its lumps, I must admit; it also had had its elevated moments. We'd traveled on cruise ships and landed in ports where my mother had never dreamed of setting foot. We had visited sites she had only known from the History Channel. Our excursions to points of interest had become commonplace. Random treks to the waterfront and a view of New York skylines always excited her; night lights and the casino glitter elevated her.

Foforito's odyssey had been one of redemption. She traveled from mud roads leading to Barranquitas to being entertained by Broadway shows and the most recognizable musicians of our times. I wondered what was occupying her mind behind her leer. Was she pensive? Did her attention provide wondrous reflection? She turned to me, apparently sensing my inquisitive stare. There was a soft tone in her voice, "You've done all you could for me. I'm grateful. You're a good son, and I love you."

I muttered, "Did God put you up to saying that?" Obviously, I was touched at this profound statement of validation, but was she setting me up? It humbled me; I paused so that I could have a moment for my slushiness to bubble over. It somehow made everything moving forward bearable.

The following months were dense and intense. Foforito's spirit had become rigid; she wasn't as fluid as in her yesteryears, or for that matter, yesterday. Her decline had been steadfast; her movements became unsure and rickety. At every turn, unwilling to accept assistance, she was confrontational and bitchy. The thought of a walker insulted her independence and hardened her resolve. My perseverance started to show some cracks, good intentions were beaten down, a malignant air consumed the quarters we shared. She kept moving about as if caught in a storm without compass or direction. Whenever dizzy spells wrestled with her wobbly stride, she would call on God's assistance. I had to substitute in *His* absence, and that was pissing me off. After all, she never lashed out at the Brother upstairs, but here she was blasting me... well, you know. Then, as if when she was most exhausted from chasing a butterfly, it came and landed on her shoulder to ease her into a calm. *SHIT! Maybe her God had stopped in when I had my guard down. Devotion had the nerve to be a trickster.*

My knees were buckling from relentlessly piercing back pain as it traveled and anchored at my toe. Cancellation of a side job (a small construction that afforded me some extra income) allowed me some time to exhale and recuperate. Additionally, my pen became a conduit to pain relief as I scribbled on my legal pad. I was parked in my car underneath a once-shady tree in Liberty State Park. A vibrant sun was hidden behind two humungous clouds that hovered over the New York skyline. From the confines of my vehicle, I watched decaying leaves clutching to their final moments. Many comrades before them lay in heaps as sacrifices to the changing of the seasons. Some remained, fighting off a wind bent on undressing the erect columns of trees. Their grasp was reminiscent of Foforito's resolve. My feelings of late lay scattered, as did the foliage, in various stages of communal desertion. I had started relationships, convinced that the common threads of interest had been clipped by my mother's scissors, which I'm sure I had handed her on occasion. Vulnerability and periods of loneliness weighing heavily on my shoulders had caused me to revisit the shortfalls of my checkered past. Those two fellas whispering in my ears were presenting valid arguments for their individual entrenched beliefs. At day's end the only question that needed a retort was, *Are you happy?* The comeback remained tangled between the wind and the hold of the falling leaves.

Liberty State Park had become a sanctuary, a place to gather myself and reaffirm that the conditions were temporary. With an internal review, I lamented the loss of those relationships that had rewarded and delivered me a genuine affection. I had fumbled, misread, or mishandled each for reasons I couldn't grasp at those junctures. What they had brought to the table in intelligence, grace, passion, and above all, honesty, had helped shape the person I'd become. Mocking myself, and in my defense, I heaped praise on myself for also bringing something of substance to the table. Commitment was the thorn that plagued me, and found me in a quagmire, even to the present time. I offered myself another vista, while beating up on Riscardo. After all, the promise I had made to assist my mother to her resting place was a commendable pledge I didn't take lightly. At times, we inadvertently take accountability for our missteps in life. Even if I didn't recognize it in the moment, ultimately, I was accountable for my own happiness. Insulated in my car, I paused to embrace the vision unfolding before me; a community of birds feasting from a Good Samaritan's generosity. The provisions caused a feeding frenzy as the birds grazed in the grass like little cows. Suddenly, they flew away, allowing me a moment's privacy with my written thoughts. How much I envied the freedom of their flight!

A view of the Hudson River's choppy waters was contradicted by the calm sky overhead. The spectacle invited tourists and locals alike to an inspired landscape of the metal and stone which defined the New York skyline. A floating sailboat braved an out-of-season adventure. In turn, I surveyed it with anchored aspirations.

The sight reminded me of my former daily drudgery and toil inside *them sky scratchers.* My aching vertebrae were testimony of my labor. It had been a period that, by sacrifice, had allowed me opportunities to travel, and learn the language of being creative. The forfeiture of my sweat was but a minor tariff for the greater good. "This too, shall come to pass," reverberated as I found my way home.

On the drive back home, I braced, as always, for unwanted catastrophe. Immediately, upon arrival, the task of surveying the messy landscape and jumping over mayhem bristled my few remaining locks. Scattered garments littered the dining area in chaos; Miriam's look told the story. Foforito had opened her suitcase, and all hell had broken loose. Screaming had caused her to hyperventilate; her tantrum had rattled Miriam. Theatre for attention was my guess. She had implored God to take her out of her misery, crying, "Me quiero morir."

Previously I had asked Miriam to try *not* to curb my

mother's outburst. "Let it take its course. If not, it will be a prerequisite for even more attention." I had jokingly assured Miriam that Foforito would not work herself into a casket.

Following my own advice, I asked, "Are you hungry? How does some rice and beans with plantains and chicken sound?" Her look said, "You bet." The flurry of activity had her famished; I would go to one of my mother's favorite eating places, located nearby, in Jersey City. In an even-toned, I instructed Foforito to "Clean up the mess" and informed her, "the food is on the way." Her discouraged reaction saddened me. Once again, unshakeable ills and misplaced thoughts emerged as permanent partners.

With Miriam's assistance, mi vieja meticulously started to relocate her belongings. I returned with the food. We devoured our portions, as the lesson to focus on something else was put behind us. Foforito found her way to the recliner; the suitcase was resigned to the closet, and Miriam escaped to the bus stop.

Smothered by the day's events, I staggered upstairs. My refuge was safeguarded by a staircase of sixteen steps which Foforito's lungs could no longer negotiate. Isolation in my makeshift dayroom was not a foolproof remedy. It was merely a hideaway, which was not necessarily the best thing for me. Swaying in the hammock provided me a sense of serenity, until a muttering sound dragged me back downstairs. Eavesdropping on her monologue, I overheard, "When the ranch is lost, all else falls apart." Quite a revelation! La Vieja was aware that the once lubricated parts were no longer fluid. She muttered the common theme of her reality, which defended her premise that she was the only sane person alive.

"Don't get old, 'cause you can't even hold your shit." Foforito's pearls of wisdom always resonated. I had mentioned to her that my birthday was right around the bend. "What can I make you?" She hadn't worked the kitchen in a bit, but I didn't discourage it. I rattled off a list of my favorite dishes.

It used to be that birthdays were cause for celebration. They were joyful markers that identified accomplishments and set goals for future jamborees. At thirteen, I had obtained working papers and started a job. At eighteen, I was able to purchase alcohol, legally; got my license to drive at twenty-one, and moved out into the world at twenty-seven. I always associated those milestones with birthdays. They earmarked my movement and highlighted my evolution. However, lately birthdays had lost the luster. Still in my heart, *I give thanks for being above ground every day. Every day becomes a gift day.* I looked in the mirror, almost fifty-eight. Shackled with mounting responsibilities, lonely, and fearful that my fall years were dwindling, I viewed my Foforito's winter of discontent. The unwanted inheritance of mannerisms and ingrained warped behavior had me exploring my resolve to shed the skin attached to them. Every day, I grappled with unpredictable circumstances that either elevated or deflated. Like the seesaw in the playground, I ended up dumping unsettled issues to one side or the other. While the middle ground—the calm, the stability—remained elusive.

Arroz con gandules, alcapurrias, and un asopao; a delicious menu. Foforito successfully lobbied for the ingredients needed for the labor-intensive dishes. Totally engaged with the project to create a feast, I made the trek to the appropriate markets with the list in hand. Excitedly, I went to the poultry man with mom's instructions. Then, I made the rounds for the many fresh condiments and herbs mandated for her recipes. When I returned, Foforito was pouting and a little agitated; fatigue was trying to obstruct her intentions. I rolled up my sleeves, emptied the shopping bags, and challenged Aida and Foforito to a battle in the kitchen. This sofrito was pureed: onions, garlic, red and green peppers were roasted, recao, cilantro, ajicitos, sea salt, ground pepper, oregano, even a pouch of prepared seasoning was added. Finally, two tablespoons of extra virgin olive oil were married into the mix. The kitchen sink was spared since it was too heavy, and too big to put into the blender. Plenty enough had been made for seasoning that meal; the excess was poured into ice trays for future recipes. The meat was cut up and cooked with the sofrito.

Foforito's head with her handkerchief crown was bobbing with a rhythm that always transformed her on these cooking adventures. She was in her element. The plantains were peeled and grated; her herb-covered hands were kneading milk and butter: it was an opera. Her arthritic fingers, resembling roots, were working the plantains into the consistency she desired. Finally, everything came together, the drums were beating—boom, boom, boom— the crescendo had reached its apex. We sat like the three tenors at the finale; contentment was etched on our faces from ear to ear. My fifty-eighth birthday became a marker, for it was one of the last performances she made in the kitchen. Going forward, whenever I entered that kitchen I was filled with gratitude for serving apprenticeship to a culinary master who made cooking into an art form: Foforito.

My mother knew how to stain a feel-good moment. That blemish had been a part of her makeup since I could recollect. My dad would give her a look at times that said, "Don't be mean." "Cut it out." Depending upon the severity, I'd pretty much become immune to her commentaries. With a swiftness, she could dig into the best intentions of others and erode the good feelings that should have been enjoyed. In these moments, Fofortito was disliking Aida, and impulsively attacking the kindly aide.

"I busted my ass so that she can benefit from my labor. She's got it good around here."

I cringed. Graciously, Aida dismissed the dagger remark, recognizing my embarrassed position for my mother's tasteless outburst. This woman had been a bedrock, allowing me space to gather myself whenever things became overbearing. At the moment Foforito was finding fault with everything Aida did to try to please her. Foforito was slinging mud again. Her trust issues with home attendants had resurfaced. Her antics were creating a strain. Foforito was doing everything to sabotage Aida's last months of work. Somehow, I had to explain to my mother the importance of cooperating; if not, there would be consequences, and they wouldn't be pretty. Hadn't we sifted through five unsatisfactory attendants before finding Aida?

After dinner and dessert, I sat Foforito down and laid the guilt trip on her with respect to Doña Aida. "If you don't approve of her, we'll fire her. What the hell? Who cares if she'll be in a bad way just before she retires?" La vieja managed to digest my diplomatic, yet firm stance and tolerated Aida for the remainder of her tenure. Rolling the rosary beads in her Christian hands, Foforito developed a concerned look as I painted a dark view of Aida's release. *Wrap that around your conscience*, I smirked inwardly. Foforito's response spoke volumes; my mother was a good person who would protect her vested interest at any cost. Dementia had wreaked havoc in her later years, but it hadn't corrupted her soul, and for that I was grateful.

Shit! I wanted a night out; just to go to a neighborhood club to hear some music. Tried not to feel the need to explain or justify my desire for "free time." Like a child slipping out the back door, I planned my getaway. I made sure all Foforito's immediate needs were within her reach. The water bottle sat on the night table; the potty was sanitized and by her side. Two rolls of toilet paper stood guard; one under the potty, the other on the lid. I removed her rosary beads, and any other usually misplaced items, then secured them in her safety box. Slippers were always placed on the right side of the bed. The checklist completed, I tiptoed to the door and made my escape. Consequently, by the time I arrived at my destination, I was so guilt-ridden that I couldn't enjoy the event at hand. Then the cloud of impending doom hovered overhead.

What if something happened in my absence?
Would I be held accountable for neglect?
Was there such a thing as elderly desertion?

I searched for a panacea and discovered paranoia. I'd become Cinderfella at the ball, and it was always midnight.

My hurried return-home steps became light as I approached the door; gingerly I opened it, fearful of what I'd find on the other side. She was sound asleep, incubated by too many covers. Sitting in my bed, I pondered my actions. *I'm fifty-eight years old and I'm sneaking out of my house like some kid. There's something wrong with this picture.* I had a good laugh at my own expense, at what in reality was no laughing matter. The writing had stopped for a while, and I felt crippled. It had been the only thing that had allowed me to really escape.

I was trapped. In a season—winter to spring—words had been replaced with plants and flowers. My mother was in her element, planting things. Mixing the soil gave her joy, and the gritty feel put a bounce in her stride. It was a bonding agent for both of us as we arranged baskets and shrubs, vines and bulbs. The uneven pieces of slate that formed the garden flooring, became a mine field in the presence of Foforito's intermittent dizzy spells and unsteady feet. She was very guarded, fearful of placing herself in harm's way, she watched and dictated directions. Barking orders like a sergeant, the only thing missing were the stripes on her house dress. Gardening was therapeutic, though, and it filled a void for the time being for both of us. With the garden in mind, I zig-zagged from the branch I was working on to the dinner table just in time to hear Foforito grumbling. She was in rare form, eager to share the valuable information brimming and ready to burst from her Johnson and Johnson cream-laced cheeks.

"Prepara el café," la vieja commanded from her comfortable seat at the table where she had primed and propped herself. I almost put my hands in the fire to accelerate the percolating process. She had promised to relate a recent dream. I got a kick out of her storytelling and didn't want the opportunity to escape her memory. Coffee cup in hand, she blew into the steamy fumes as they tickled her nose. Foforito wanted to reveal her dream in detail. I knew the telling would be a stimulating curve that would heighten her sense of being.

Squinting her eyes, she began telling the dream... trudging so many steps, with no clue of their destination. They were all in a single direction leading to a murky and fuzzy place she couldn't make out. Reliving how the rise and the tread had exhausted her in the dream, caused her to pause the telling. She sipped on her coffee and caught her breath before she resumed the adventurous dream climbing. After a few pit stops, she reached the pinnacle of an elevated horizon. Her detailed accounts of the surreal imagery were piquing my interest. No longer as an act of courtesy, I was listening intently; she had my undivided attention.

She had come to swirling ornamental gates. Her transparent telling allowed me to view the artistry of the blacksmith through her inspecting eyes. She said the gates were not confining, they were an entryway to a welcoming, peaceful place. In her dream and still, now, they left her awestruck. She became animated as she recounted the events.

"I saw your father... and your brother."

All those souls pushing up the daisies.

She was painting a Picasso right before my eyes. As she went to enter, the gatekeeper, anchored in duty to protect the place of serenity, appeared stern and unyielding. Against her wishes to join her husband and her son, Foforito was directed back to the dreaded steps. The voice of her present reality echoed to her about unfinished business at steps' end. Turning her back on the decorated doorway, she left dejected. The ambulated descent was draining; She had been robbed of fulfilling her desire to embrace those dear to her. Her disappointment was evident in her confabulation. She had to return to the mess, to sort out what was left to do in the here and now. I sat in my seat amused; and exhausted.

"WOW!" The tale was tantalizing, and I must admit her storytelling moved me. I looked at her with a serious-minded eye and locked into her still-excited gaze. Full of emotion and wanting to disentangle her from the mystery and disappointment of it all, I hugged her. Grabbing her arthritic limbs in mine, I held her close to my chest; mutually, we exhaled.

Attempting to lighten the mood, I started up. "You go tell that gatekeeper I'll take care of everything down here. He needn't worry about a thing. You tell him that all's well in this here present. You go back up them steps; I know it's tough, but you give him that message loud and clear." I knew she couldn't hear my remarks or appreciate the observations of the vortex of her memory. I laughed internally at my lampooning moment. The story remained attached like belly fat. There was unfinished business which needed inspection, so that her transition, when it arrived, would be without complication or regret. I also felt privileged that I, for whatever reason, had been chosen to escort her to that place when the gatekeeper called.

CLOSURE

AFTER AN EXTENDED PERIOD OF INCARCERATION,
my pen received a reprieve. A liberated air replaced the
smothered sense of what I would uncover as I confronted
this memoir's final chapter. Fear was converted to fuel. I
had struggled with the thought of placing my mother in a
nursing facility as the final stages of her illnesses became
apparent.

That reality was gut-wrenching and fragile. It had me
wavering in an uneasy space. Guilt was presenting itself
opportunistically, as reason countered the harm's way my
girl was in, here in our home. The steps leading down to
the kitchen or up to her sleeping quarters had gone from
being a source of exercise to an instrument of torment.
The gossipy gaze she had once used from her nest at the
window had become a blank stare. I hadn't promised her
a rose garden, and yet she was presented with that and
more. The cluster of plants inside the window surrounded
her, while roses elevated by the sun and rain neighbored
on the other side of the glass.

Camouflaged and lurking, she entertained herself with
passersby—school-bound, work-bound, bus-bound, or
out of bounds. Now relegated to watch, she envied others
their active state. The sun wrestled past the foliage and
wooden blinds to highlight Foforito's white locks. Before

my eyes the sunset painted a halo to crown the portrait she became sitting in the coffee niche. At day's end, she dreaded preparation for ascent to her sleeping area. I walked behind her hugging her with encouragement. She peered up, viewing the inevitable, and then with fragile steps started her climb.

Foforito paused in mid-stride, searching for a youthful breath now buried under years of unrewarded toil. Her antique energy was fossil fuel which evaporated with every attempt forward. "Bajando está, la calabasa llega," she murmured, as she parked herself between steps.

La Vieja looked over her shoulder gasping for air, COPD chocking away at her earnest attempts for air. In a helpless gaze, she proclaimed that she would get tired watching water run, a fitting statement for the moment at hand. She could be so eloquent at times. I encouraged her movement. "You're going to miss the Yankee game." The thought rejuvenated her, as she did her version of scampering up the steps. "Getting old sucks," kept reverberating as she proclaimed victory at the last step. She slumped into her butaca, honed by years of usage, to accommodate her shrinking frame. Pleading for a glass of water, she struggled with the erratic cadence of her heart's beat.

Things were starting to unravel in my own body rapidly; the sciatic nerve went from pecking to pounding, to crippling. Each step became a needling reminder of limitations and exhausted duty. A full-frontal view captured a deflated posture reminiscent of a prize fighter doubled over the time-out stool. Baggage had settled like squatters under glazed eyes; my own image startled me.

Draining days were consumed with lobbying for

additional service hours for my mother. This pilgrimage was laden with relinquishments. We needed help. My energy was tapped to the limit as I battled to contain the exploitive diseases that were mounting daily within my aged warrior body. Nights were no longer periods of resuscitation, as recurring nightmares highjacked my moments of inactivity. The head-butting with my marble mantle, the picking up of scattered ornaments, rewound and repeated.

One morning, I was chased into darkness and evicted into rude awakening as the chase came to its destination. The wake-up lunge found me splattered on a cold, hard-ass floor next to the bed. My shoulder received the brunt of the damage and following the fall I grimaced as the sciatic nerve decided to partner in torturing me. I managed a call to Gloria and her nephew Felipe my good friends, who could immediately assist me, until Lourdes, my mother's Saturday caretaker, reported for duty.

Finally, able to leave home, I drove myself to the ER for x-rays. Luckily, contusions were the only damages. When I arrived home from the hospital, the motherly concern etched on Foforito's face was telling, "If something happens to you, something happens to me."

Bearing witness, by way of inspection, she was drenched with emotion framed in helplessness. In between sobs, she offered to make some chicken soup. "I don't have a cold," I replied, breaking a tension that had accelerated our heartbeats. My threshold for pain crossed to critical during that period and caused me to take a hard look at my circumstances.

Mom's home attendant, Miriam stayed with us for two

weeks during my recovery. Even as I write, I have a debt of gratitude for her service in that period of uncertainty. In a devastated heap, saturated with liabilities, I had become irritable and unpleasant. Disabled and dependent on others for my needs, I was also despondent: not a pretty picture.

Eventually, I began to thaw from that unfamiliar and distasteful place. An inner resolve elevated itself, as I, a self-proclaimed, fair-weather atheist, reluctantly started exercising the power of prayer to forces unknown at that moment in time. My mood started to mend. The evolution of circumstances humbled me. During kneeling moments of despair my atheist view reflected... *Are spirituality and religion one and the same?* I stepped outside the vortex, stopped moping, and began my climb. Pain became bearable; the light of day provided me another outlook. I ventured to the garden and witnessed new life sprouting from perennials. That instant redirected my movement forward.

Time mandated it was not *if;* but when. My mother's visiting nurse, as well as the social worker, urged me to at least entertain the idea of placing Foforito in a nursing facility. Her doctor also broached that premise. I wrestled with their suggestions for a good while; hemming and hawing until I started to do the paperwork necessary to move the process forward.

In taking that course of action, I entered one of the most difficult periods of my life. It was becoming crystal clear that honoring tradition was going to fall short of its intended goal. Foforito, at ninety-four, needed twenty-four hour supervision which impaired this journey's wishes, as

I was ill-equipped to provide that service. Her heart was in a delicate condition after what was labeled as a minor heart attack, as if any heart attack can be dismissed as minor. She also had COPD and other pulmonary diseases. Dementia and her hearing problems were major because it further diminished her ability to communicate. Those sweatshop sewing machines had done a number on her over the years. Foforito was becoming brittle; the battles were many, and her armor was shredded. My squeaky-clean mother was even refusing to bathe. Her chest pains, both real and imagined, were daily complaints that would, on occasion, cause an ambulance visit; some of the technicians knew her on a first name basis. Numerous emergency room visits and hospital stays followed. Her ornery and commendably defiant spirit became a grind for her as we moved towards imminent resolution.

Boom! I heard her scream for help. Lately, I was on high alert due to her increasingly frail state. She had fallen trying to sit on the potty and was making a messy effort to reach the bathroom on the lower level. I caught her in mid-stride; she insisted on using the bathroom downstairs. After placing her on the bowl, I started picking up the trail of feces. Foforito reluctantly submitted to a sponge bath, I removed her soiled housedress, got her slippers, and powdered her tender anal area. Then I wrapped her up in a fresh bata. The trek back to her room bankrupted her formerly zestful efforts as her tiny frame, by now under one hundred pounds, slid onto her bed. Those moments were but a privileged few; I felt honored to be in that position. I hugged her, feeling the fragile state of her being in the fold of my arms. She thanked me as her arthritic fingers ruffled the sparse strands of hair clinging to my scalp. "Que Dios te bendiga, m'ijo." I started warming up to the idea of the nursing facility; my internal debate sparring with it at every turn.

La Vieja adamantly refused to take any medication, so I became vigilant at pill-popping time. She would fake the swallow, and then bury the meds into the soil on the window ledge. Like a good defense lawyer, she pointed to the sorry-looking plant. "Look at what they're doing to the plant, I'm not taking them." Upon closer review, the wilted leaves had appeared to be a casualty of those toxic chemicals. Her argument was persuasive, maybe she was right... I went upstairs to my bed.

Tick, tock. At two o'clock in the morning, I gave up the struggle with my pillow to negotiate for some much-needed rest. I ventured to Foforito's room to find her absent from bed. Another flight downstairs to the kitchen, and there she was in her designated spot, oblivious of her surroundings. Her distant stare into the night lights captured an occasional car on its way. Having attempted to prepare herself a meal, she now sat hidden inside the shadow of darkness, accompanied by scavengers pecking away at garbage bags and leftover treats. She struck up a conversation with herself that became confrontational. A hard-boiled egg in the kitchen had exploded and eggshell fragments were embedded in the ceiling and walls. Milk coated the stove and the burner like porcelain.

The thought of not having risen when I did had me a little rattled. I interrupted her moment of meditation and brought the negligence and my concerns to her attention. Immediately she denied any responsibility and pointed an accusing finger in my direction. Easy-Off spray fumes hovering in the air put a kink in my thinking and the decisions moving forward. I was sure her childhood had played a significant role in her not wanting to accept responsibility when things went bad. These survival skills were surely fine-tuned as her defense mechanisms. That my home was becoming a minefield was forcing my hand with unpleasant decisions.

Not good enough. Not good. No, no. I visited several facilities, always finding fault with them. The only residence I viewed as possibly suitable was near my home. Additionally, many of the residents and staff spoke Spanish. Foforito had been there for rehab on a couple of occasions, and the staff knew me. All the same, there would be challenges; my mother wouldn't take this lightly. Completely clueless on how to present it to her, I didn't want Foforito to feel I was punishing her in any way.

At a glance, I could separate the transient patients, only there on rehab assignments, as opposed to those sentenced as permanent dwellers. Residents strapped to wheelchairs, betrayed by memory, sat in formation like heaps of dirty laundry. *A sad metaphor as even I write it.* Several stared with anxious eyes seeking attention or craving casual conversation. Worse, too, many wore blank expressions; the proverbial folks 'lost at sea.' The image hurt my heart and cursed my words. *What the fuck is going on here?* When I sat with a social worker there, she mentioned, with cold indifference, that a waiting period would likely outlast Foforito's need to be placed in the facility. Immediately, I realized I would have to be diligent on my mother's behalf.

I became discouraged by her callous remark, which I found to be void of professionalism or compassion, and quite defiant, to boot. Her pointless chatter pounded away at my purpose. I mostly ignored her voice, until I heard her ask, "Are you okay?" I recoiled, gathered myself and handed her the paperwork, which I had filled out prior to speaking with her. She reviewed the paperwork and complimented me on my diligence. I disregarded her praise; she had already shitted on herself. I had simply wanted my mother to be placed on the waiting list. Referring to the application in her hand, the social worker asked, "Is this your best contact number?" To which I replied, "Don't worry, I'll be a pest," as I exited the nursing facility.

Filing my heels against the pavement, I searched for direction. Finally, I called Foforito's primary care doctor. Foforito's troubling list of afflictions was mounting daily.

Slumped in my car for whatever reason, I felt sorry for the lady who had just tried to derail my objective. It had to have been horrible dealing with the daily downhill slide of the aging, a cruel reminder of what was inevitable should one attain that status in seniority. The memory of that day room remained a contentious place for me, as it drained my outlook. My line of business had always left callouses of physical residue. But those who work in elder-care facilities, by choice or by default, must develop a thick skin of the heart or fall victim to the pain of indifference.

The phone rang; it was the doctor returning my call. I explained my dilemma. He listened to my run-on sentence. Before I could exhale, he gave me the direction which devastated me.

"Take her to the emergency room, she'll be admitted for three days, and then transferred to the facility that you have chosen where she'll remain as a permanent resident. It's best for her. Good luck."

My jaw dropped. I had been stubbornly in denial. I hadn't prepared myself for the directive I had received; it came crashing down on me like a sack of rancid potatoes. Blindsided and dazed, the question for me then was, *What to do next?* I was overcome with guilt. My memory fled to the past. *Eugenia.* My grandmother was with us until I was eleven and she was eighty-four. We were joined at the hip until she expired. All our elders had been cared for. *I stumbled at the finish line. Traditional customs were being compromised on my watch.*

Foforito had laid pangs of conscience on me. They hadn't wanted another child. "I decided to have you against the wills of others," she would frequently tell me. That information had tangled with my ability to reason and make sense of it all now, nearing her Judgment Day. Indecision was about to render me inadequate.

The weight of proxy overwhelmed me as I confronted pent-up emotions. I pressed the release valve, allowing my sentiments to fill the rims of my camouflaging glasses. I thanked the doctor for his service, and then sat in the moment, digesting all that was to follow. I called Miriam, made her aware of what was imminent, and asked her to dress my mother.

Miriam had been wonderful to us and had become the daughter my mother never had. She had dressed Foforito to the nines and transformed her into a picture of perfect health. My proud, tiny bundle of joy looked like she was ready for a casino visit. She could be so huggable when not ornery, rare those days.

"Where are we going?" I was overcome with emotion; my eyes provided a murky view of her innocence. My lips quivered as composure betrayed me. "To see the doctor," surprised that I was able to communicate, given my state of mind. She clutched her purse, "I'm hungry and I'm paying."

We headed to her favorite eatery. The owner and the employers knew her well, treated her with reverence and pampered her with attention. She responded like the ham she could be. The owner's compliment to me touched a personal nerve, "You're a good son, I wish I still had my mother."

That statement drained me; my appetite evaporated. A half a bowl of soup littered the table, as Foforito and I wrestled over the bill. The short drive felt like a procession as we made our way to the ER. The diagnosis was that she had an irregular heartbeat and a small urinary tract infection. It relieved me that they discovered that and treated it accordingly.

Driving back from the hospital was a blur; the entanglement of emotions had wrecked me. A view in the mirror reflected a sunken figure. "Dead man walking" was a fitting description as I separated myself from the car. I had taken a 'one-two punch' and was on wobbly legs. My defeated posture was testimony to internal bickering. A decision was being made; one that my mother never could have a voice in, and worse, one that she was unaware of. In my head were the voices of aborted embryos, her decision to have me; my sense of duty undermined by circumstance. Those voices were deafening. My abode was no longer equipped to accommodate her needs, and she was in harm's way. I had to reconcile that. And yet, the taste of betrayal filled my mouth.

I gagged as I fumbled with the keys at the entryway. Miriam was a mess. After bonding with her for such a time, this abrupt severance was raw and difficult to digest. These two domino partners were separated by my course of action; and so, the pieces were falling.

Over the next few days, I made back-and-forth runs to the hospital with food and treats I knew she loved. The dinner was her favorite, since she'd get the Italian pastries. The orgasmic groans after she devoured one would resonate. In less than a week, I received news that she was being transferred to the rehab facility. That news reignited the scepter condemnation.

The accommodations were straightforward: two beds, one bathroom, two dresser draws and two privacy curtains. Foforito developed a quick friendship with her roommate, Doña Maria; they became buddies. Their conversations were shouting matches since both were nearly deaf. Unfortunately, Mom took a tumble on the way to the bathroom, became a fall-risk, and was transferred to Room 518, next to the nurses' station. It became her last place of residence. Every day Foforito would ask, "When will I be going home?" I ran out of excuses, "Soon, when you get better... when you're a little stronger... any day now."

The visits were excruciating, every day a reminder that I had been derelict in cultural duty. She was usually parked in the dayroom, surrounded by folks in similar circumstances. But every day I was present and accountable with morning coffee and oatmeal or an afternoon soup. Each time I arrived and smothered her with affection, kissing and pecking until she fought off my advances. If she saw me in the hallway, she'd scream, "Mi hijo!", throwing her hands in the air as if she was doing the wave at a ballpark. It would startle her comrades. The gesture in part, as I took it, was calculated to make them envious. Over time, I convinced myself that Riscardo had made the right choice, even as my emotions still found a platform for debate.

Wheeling my girl to her quarters, we would find mutual ground for entertainment—*Jeopardy, Wheel of Fortune,* and the Yankee games. She couldn't hear or understand any of the games, but it was someone to cheer for or against. After a few innings, the TV watched her.

Foforito internalized the residence as our home and asked me if I was going upstairs to sleep. On the one hand, I was relieved and less stressed about her physical comfort. However, there were still unresolved issues and resentments that had festered and would no longer have a soapbox for expression. I realized in the cramped quarters of her room in the new residence, that the opportunity to share with her that which had worn at me for some time, had slipped away.

Perhaps what clawed at me and made me cringe the most was the "unwanted child" theme when she felt insecure. Rejection had been a point of contention for me; the angst whenever someone exposed their affection in her presence was always a cause of concern. I'd felt a need to protect the well-intended embraces and shield them from her attacks.

That unpaid debt was stained by obsession and layers of guilt. That I had been made was a mistake. All that raw shit tangled up like the needlepoint threads, would always engage her at day's end. I'd come to realize that our childhood holds the key to our happiness, if we recognize the sins of our innocence. I continued to chisel away at my inheritance, separating the muck from the wholesome intent, and the talents she perfected. I guess we're each a work in progress.

Her decline was like pages in a book; as each page was turned, the conclusion came closer. She enjoyed the rubdowns. Her tender back, fragile to touch, received more delicate strokes; her legs, no longer supportive, were kneaded now with caution. Her feet welcomed the massages and were afforded special attention. She looked forward to those chapters as the pages caught wind.

When I'd change her diaper and powder what remained of her buttocks, she at last recognized that as an act of compassion. I was just reciprocating what she had done lovingly as a parent. I had learned what it took to raise one. "Hey baby, you cleaned my butt, so I'll wipe yours." Foforito went from embarrassment to acceptance as our remaining moments started to thaw.

Entering her bathroom, I immediately had a flashback. At the tender age of twelve, without warning, I had barged into the bathroom to relieve my bladder. Chuito was already there, planning to shave his face of a two-day growth. I lifted the lid of the bowl and wedged myself attempting for privacy. In preparation, Dad had placed the Gillette blade on the sink, mixed the soap into a foam, and lathered his face. Not at all a tall fellow, he and I were head to head in the head. The view he caught amused him. Finishing my business, I shook it twice, flipped it in, zipped, put the lid down, flushed and was ready to exit.

"Hey," he bellowed from the foam that encircled his lips, "you're not done yet." "What?" I replied. He lifted the lid and told me to fetch a tissue to clean both the seat and the rim. I did what I was told and was ready to scamper. Again, he reprimanded, "Hey, you're still not done. Wash your hands, Mister."

Damn! I thought. *I'm not operating on anyone.* Then he sat me on the seat. "You will marry someday, and if you don't practice proper hygiene, your wife could get a urinary tract infection." He chuckled, "You won't get any action." "Besides, your mother lives here... and we still have our moments." A smile rose above the foam. In parting he told me, "Next time, knock."

Foforito's efforts to and from the bathroom became labor intensive, getting out the wheelchair zapped her energy. She resembled a novice on skates, but she clung to those remnants of independence, a feat I found beyond commendable. Performing simple procedures, which could liberate the elderly of the need for antibiotics, proved to be not so readily available, especially in understaffed nursing facilities, however well-intentioned they might be. I cleaned the bowl and changed her undergarments nightly. She'd be ready in the event she dreamt of my dad.

Jokingly, as humor was always in my pocket, I asked the reluctant Florence Nightingales if they had any wheelchairs with ejector buttons. We had a system down pat, utilizing the grab bars and encouragement. The battle was rewarded with the impression of self-reliance.

Foforito's sock-sandals served as swivels to place her back in the bed. She would land like a papaya parachuting from a tree; then, I'd give her a double high-five, complimenting her fortitude and success. Shortly, that method of using the bathroom facilities became obsolete as my mom's frail condition increasingly worsened.

On a lighter note, Foforitos' last bathroom adventure, with me as her faithful assistant did take on a humorous twist. After she had relieved herself, I knelt in the confined space in front of the commode. I proceeded, foolishly, to put on her diaper-garment as she hinged off the grab bar with one hand, while the other held up the bata around her stomach. As I fumbled with the Velcro fastening tab, the nurse arrived. La vieja let go of the bata and draped it around my head like a turban. The nurse, amused, asked if she could be of assistance. It was a lighthearted moment that remains a treasure.

Soon thereafter, I reached out to family near and far to let them know time was in short supply. Her decline now had a sprinter's legs. It would be a good idea to visit while she was still lucid. The well-wishers she had touched were front and center, filling her quarters with their sentiments. My Uncle Benny, his daughter Susie and her husband Rob; Ganya with her family; Gibran with his; Cathy, Teresa, Yolanda, all were present and accounted for. Room 518 was transformed into a perfumed space where stories of gratitude mingled with bouquets of flowers. That outpouring of support reenergized my efforts. April 1, 2013, her ninety-fifth birthday shindig was a blast, as friends and family celebrated her status as matriarch. She marinated in the attention and shoveled ice cream and cake to her heart's content. It was to become her last joyous meal.

Days later, a meeting with the social worker exposed my mother's prognosis. Her loss of appetite further complicated bleak circumstances. A feeding tube was offered as an option. Being my mother's health proxy, I had more decisions to make. I reached out to Al and asked for his opinion on the matters at hand. His response was parallel with mine; his statement poetic and laced with sentiment. "Don't take the spoon out of her hand."

After a number of years together, Al and Yolanda had planned a formal ceremony to celebrate their union. They were getting married in a week; Foforito was in a downward spiral. I called to update Al about this dilemma and hatch possible solutions. Foforito already in hospice care was resting comfortably, but there was really no telling how long she would hold on. Meanwhile, people were flying to the wedding from Pittsburgh, New York, North Carolina, Arizona, Sacramento. It was a perfect storm. I suggested to Al to stay put. I'd make the necessary arrangements here, take a flight out west the day before the wedding and return back east as soon as possible. A cloud of impending doom hovered like a neurotic drone. I separated Foforito's attire and mine, dropped them off at the cleaners, went home and reviewed my next steps.

Ordinarily, arm in arm Foforito and I would arrive at these functions, her little hands clutching my sleeves. I had always admired her tiny creative fingers, now wrinkled, twisted and mangled by time. Little nails always cropped, never manicured, pampered or painted. Creative hands she used to meticulously inspect her personal wardrobe. With loving affection those same hands had ruffled my hair in my youth; or beat me with her chancletas when I stepped out of line. Those hands spoke volumes if one is attuned to that alphabet. A white blouse she had handcrafted with a detailed bib from her neck to her bust, was chosen. It was her favorite. A simple black vest and black polyester pants completed the ensemble which would accompany her to her maker. I had almost forgotten the elusive bra and Clorox-white underwear that had wreaked havoc in my life for the past thirty years. I handed Ms. Brominski, the funeral director, my mother's apparel, a check and the necessary paperwork to jump-start the process. Black suit in hand, I stepped onto the plane with a heavy heart, and enough personal articles to hold me over for the next few days. Generally, globally, weddings and funerals are magnets for family gatherings. That season, for our family, they were bookends as well.

Al picked me up at the airport; the rest of the clan had either arrived or were en route. We headed to the motel where we settled into the room that would house us until he recited, "I do." The dress rehearsal was held at the church, and later that night, most of us who had migrated to southern California for the wedding could be found splashing in the pool. Every call on my cell phone had me on edge, although when the phone remained silent, it was also cause for concern. As if on schedule, my friend for almost fifty years, Delaney, called to share the news of his mother's passing. It saddened me to not be in position to embrace him in his moment of sorrow. His mother, Eva, had been like a mother to me whenever I made my way to her home.

In the midst of my internal strife, I was touched by little Joey, my niece's son. It seemed as if he could see my troubled thoughts and eased me into calm. First, he offered a towel, as I was shivering from both the disturbing news and the cool evening temperatures. Then he offered me a neck massage. I saw in his eyes a look that said, "It's going to be okay."

Family and friends gathered to bear witness. The happy couple exchanged vows, and the reception went well. Before my "best man" speech, I asked everyone in attendance to pray for Foforito who was on the threshold of transitioning, even as we celebrated Yolanda and Al's marriage. I spoke of and gave praise to the two folks, Chuito y Foforito, whose love ultimately made the present moment possible. Camp by camp I filled my camera with family photos.

Then I spent the next two days in complete stress overload, trying to rebook my flight across the country from the Pacific to the Atlantic. My cousin Junior, who lives next to where Foforito was resting, called and advised that I should find my way back home sooner than later. In a frustrating interaction with one of the airlines, my emergency clashed with their business ethics. So, another airline became the alternate choice by default. Yogui picked me up at the airport; I picked up my car and was subsequently denied midnight entry into the nursing facility.

The following morning, I rushed to her side. Foforito was resting; morphine dripped into her from the intravenous tube attached to her arm. Strategic cushions were placed in various locations for her comfort. Foforito appeared ashy and drawn, her skin painted onto her bones, absent of muscle tone. Her gaze was distant, but not vacant. She looked in my direction, and I could see the excitement in them. She whispered, "M'ijo," recognizing me. I knelt to kiss her, and she mustered enough pep for her lips to return a smooch, faint yet tender.

It meant the world to me that she hung in there. It was also the last time her eyes smiled. Al and Yolanda were finding their way. I picked them up at the airport, and we headed straight to the residence. Al's ailing knees buckled, and his emotions were raw. I'm sure there had been unresolved issues bottled up like fermented wine. We can cloak ink spots by wearing black shirts, but it is best perhaps to rid ourselves of the leaky pen. It was time to deal with the matters at hand. We clung to her side for the remaining four days of her life, the last one tattooed into my mind.

When we arrived at her bedside, Foforito was struggling, her breath challenged and erratic. Each gasp was weaker; yet each gasp defiant. Her skin tone was changing as the oxygen failed to find its way. The warrior in her was doing battle as she was being reeled in. I sponged her lips with water and told her she was not alone. I whispered, "It's okay to let go."

Miriam arrived as Foforito started to surrender; Yolanda stood guard on one side, I on the other. I leaned in and whispered into her ear, "Always remember in your heart that you remain in mine."

Foforito expired, on Monday, June 24th, 2013, on a bright sunny day, surrounded by folks who loved her. She had known and carried me for the ten months before I was born; she heard my first cry. It was only fitting that I witnessed her last breath. Foforito had fought the good fight. I was relieved that her pain was finished. Al returned from a smoke break as we marinated in communal grief.

The next few days were manageable since arrangements had been previously addressed. The standing-room-only crowd moved me as I readied to bury my mother. Ganya, her grandchild, gave an eloquent eulogy. Nancy (a very dear friend who was about to relocate to Australia) had prepared a keepsake program with pictures that captured Foforito's personality. One by one, folks spoke of Foforito with reverence. The memento prayer card we distributed beautifully framed my mother's wedding picture and put everything into perspective. The cemetery was, as always, a doleful place, but there was some comfort in reintroducing my parents.

EPILOGUE

The dust was settling. I could still hear the click-clack clatter of her chancletas and smell the lingering aroma of her culinary talents in my commandeered kitchen. Maja soap still perfumed her drawer. Above the chest of drawers, I built shelves to relocate the rosary-draped altar Foforito had created from her keepsakes and pictures of Chuito and Tony. These mementos and my ongoing treks to the cemetery remain as part of my connection to three wonderful souls.

A few months after Foforito's passing, I mustered the wherewithal to review her belongings. I donated her wardrobe to acquaintances and various religious institutions in the community. Although, I kept one of her bras just in case of resurrection, *one never knows*. I contacted family and friends who would appreciate some of her handmade tapestries which always kept her creatively entertained. These and some other of her possessions were distributed as heirlooms. I searched for the powder case which housed her gambling money; the faces of my parents on their wedding day were on the face of the case. In any case, my mother's good luck charm had mysteriously disappeared—either misplaced or worse, confiscated by one of her many attendants.

During those dust-settling months, I took a trip to Puerto Rico and drove to Barranquitas and Comerio, to speak to my Uncle Benny and Aunt Eloisa, my mother's closest siblings. My mission was to ask them what they might know about my mother's period of servitude in Philadelphia. She had always been dismissive when I broached that subject. Convenient amnesia kept that information forever clandestine. There remained a guarded secret which I suspected had crippled her emotionally. In the back of my mind, I knew sometimes silence speaks volumes. I hoped Benny and Eloisa would break that silence. They didn't. So, I was left to assume. Assumptions can wreak havoc in our lives.

The next day, on the same visit to Puerto Rico I traveled along the autopista for two hours to the other side of the island. That day's mission was to visit an elder, Doña Provi (Denise's distant relative, who happened to have the same name as my maternal grandmother). Then in her mid-nineties, Doña Provi had been relegated to a makeshift nursing facility. Cotín, my father-in-law, saddled with dementia, rode shotgun next to me, singing. His selected tunes were reminiscent of a forgotten period. Songs had been penned with perfume and laced with poetry, as he exercised his diluted memory with phrases that defined his heyday. In the back seat were Denise, her mother (Doña Lydia), and Angel Luis (Doña Lydia's boyfriend). Indeed, we were a crew!

When we arrived at the facility Doña Provi had been so sedated that her head was animated on her neck like a bobble doll. Excessive make-up had been applied to her face; I supposed in efforts to disguise the realities of her aging, including inadequate caretaking, and her response to those realties. The exaggerated paint made her face look like a frightened clown. Cotín placed his hands on her cheeks and kissed her crown above a brow wrinkled with over seventy years of remembrance. A brief visit, so revolting, I went outside to throw up. During the ride back with Denise's tribo, my deflated spirit searched for answers.

Cotín pressed the rewind button. "What's today's date?" became his redundant theme. Everything about that day—the visit, the car ride, the company—caused me to wrangle with the decision I had made following the doctor's directive to take my mother to the ER for the final time. Could I ever reconcile that the elder-care facilities, however well-intended they may try to be, nonetheless, undermine the independence, dignity and self-respect that folks work so hard to achieve? Not all facilities, but in too many not to mention. Moving forward, I have tried to go forward without remorse.

Having certain inquires answered by Benny and Eloisa would have gone a long way in my understanding what had shaped my mother. I tried to shake the assumptions but still had questions. Why my mother's disdain for her mother? Foforito, had escorted Doña Provi through her final days in the respected and traditional fashion. And what about the pictures from my mother's youth—they never showed a smile? Foforito had been a warrior, one whose childhood had been ambushed. She had been indentured so others could reap her harvest. Could that explain her contempt for her younger siblings who had benefitted from her sacrifices, as they enjoyed things she was denied—personal time, formal education?

As an innocent, unprotected young woman in servitude, had she been molested? More than once? Were the bitter remarks that consumed her dialogues a way of retaliation for the torment of unprovoked attacks? I recalled that she never wore a bathing suit, nor painted her nails. She shunned the attention wearing seductive, alluring clothing caused and was critical of anyone who dressed or behaved provocatively. Is that why she never even ventured to dance? Understanding what had shaped and misshaped Foforito may have also supported the search for my own emotional DNA.

"...The roads to el campo have been buried
with concrete which wear away
eating our fragile emotional souls
as we seek to search out our true identities..."

I struggled with myself when people asked if I missed Foforito; as if missing someone validates your feelings for them or lessens the void. The pages of my life continued to turn. Eight months to the day after my mother's passing, I finished this memoir, in Australia, of all places. Sometimes we need to travel to distant corners of the globe to discover what has been sitting inside all along.

September 2017, four years after my mother had passed, Huracán María ravaged the northeastern Caribbean. Puerto Rico, my mother's homeland was devasted. I traveled there for various reasons. While I was there, Doña Lydia asked me if I would relocate the bed my mother had used on her visits to the island. When I shifted the bed, the powder case slipped out from underneath the mattress. My knees buckled with emotion, I felt as if the hurricane had unearthed the powder case and landed it in my lap. Finding the illusive heirloom exorcised some of my remaining tears. I also asked the powers that be to forgive me for thinking ill of those caretakers who I had considered suspect. The case is now on Foforito's altar in my home. It has come full circle.

Today with my pen, I bury petty resentments, and render invisible the wounds and the scars they left. Today, I liberate myself of unsettled matters that could cloud my compass. Today and henceforth, I embrace love, and in doing so understand that forgiveness and love are inseparable.

While alive, Foforito's spirit sometimes seemed unforgiving. At the time of her transition, I sensed that her spirit remained unsettled. As we laid Foforito to rest, perhaps most troubling for me, was the thought that she had taken with her an agonizing shame, she had never been able to abort. I pray that Foforito—from daughter to matriarch—and her ascended spirit has forgiven... soaring in dance.

———

APPENDIX

GLOSSARY

WORDS

abrazo:	hug
abuela:	grandmother
adoquines:	paving stone; cobblestones
ajicitos, recao, cilantro:	ingredients for making sofrito
arroz con gandules:	rice and pigeon peas
alcapurrias:	meat patty
asopao soup:	hearty stew often includes chicken and rice
Barranquitas:	small mountain town in central Puerto Rico
batarobe:	dressing gown
batatas:	sweet potatoes
bodega:	grocery store
bendicion:	Blessing
boleros:	ballads
butacas:	bulky armchair for one person
carpetas:	carpets
caso cerrado:	case closed
Caso Cerrado:	title of a Spanish TV program
chancletas y chancletazos:	slippers and beatings with a slipper

chicharrón:	fried, seasoned meat skin (usually pork)
clave:	musical rhythm and beat
cojones:	man's balls
colador:	culinary sock with a handle used for straining
Comerío:	municipality in central Puerto Rico
consejos:	advice, suggestions
cuentos:	stories
cuero:	skin
El Diario y La Prensa:	Spanish-language newspapers
Escambrón:	beach in San Juan, Puerto Rico
flan:	custard dessert
hijo, (mi hijo, m'hijo)...:	son, (my son...)
Isle Verde:	province in Puerto Rico adjacent to San Juan airport
Juana Diaz:	municipality of Puerto Rico located in the southern coast
Mama Juana:	beverage from the Dominican Republic prepared with tree bark and herbs soaked in rum
manzanilla:	chamomile
nalgas:	a butt; a rear-end
Naranjito:	municipality in central Puerto Rico
pasteles:	African inspired dish of boiled or fried plantain leaf packets filled with meat and spices
Piñones:	town in between Carolina and Loiza in Puerto Rico
quiosco:	kiosk (small restaurant)

Ruta 3:	Route 3
sofrito:	aromatic, eclectic mix of herbs
Titi:	Aunty
tribo:	tribe (slang for family or group)
vieja, (la vieja):	elderly woman, (the elderly woman)
yuca:	a root vegetable

PHRASES & SENTENCES

page 12	Muchacho, esto me tiene debir de verda.	Boy, this has me really weak.
page 39	No te veo, mi hijo; me voy.	I can't see you, my son; I'm fading.
page 40	Estoy huerfano.	I am an orphan.
page 45	No estoy fria y ya me estan tirando la tierra.	I'm not cold and you're throwing dirt on me already.
page 49	Que Dios te bendiga.	May God bless you.
page 75	...como dos sapos de latrina	...like two latrine frogs
page 78	Aqui, todo bien.	Everything is good, here.
page 79	P'alante todo el tiempo. (Slang for para alante)	Always forward.
page 85	Tranquila, Mamita.	Easy, Mommy.

page 104	El diablo sabe mas por viejo que por diablo.	The devil knew more by being old than by being the devil.
page 128	Quires café?	Do you want coffee?
page 129	Muerto quire misa?	Does a dead person want a Mass?
page 130	Tu esta loco	You are crazy!
page 130	...lo mismo	...the same
page 138	Ay bendito.	Woe is me.
page 148	Que haces?	What are you doing?
page 168	Me quiero morir.	I want to die.
page 173	Prepara el café.	Make the coffee
page 178	Bajando está, la calabasa llega.	Going downhill even the pumpkins find their way.

UN POEMA PARA FOFORITO
Por Riscardo Alvarado

———•———

CHANCLETAS Y CHANCLETAZOS LA BENDICIÓN Y UN ABRAZO

TIENE HAMBRE

OYE MUCHACHO UN BOFETÓN UN COCOTAZO UN
   CHANCLETAZO

HARD LOVE IN A HARD TOWN IN SOME HARD TIMES

NON-NEGOTIABLE RULES AND REGULATIONS

EL MENÚ DE ARROZ BLANCO Y HUEVOS FRITOS AL CABALLO
   CON SPAM

INVENTADO POR UN BORICUA INVENTANDO EN UNA COCINA

LIVING ON THE BORDER OF THE LOWER ECONOMIC SCALE

HELPED TO HEIGHTEN THE LEVEL OF OUR CREATIVITY

FISH FRIDAYS FISH STORIES OR JUST PLAIN FISH HEAD SOUP

SORRY LOOKING CHICKENS TRYING TO COP A PLEA AT EL
   VIVERO

OR FRESH PIGEONS PARA TUMBAR UN RESFRIADO

BECAME A SPECIAL SATURDAY MORNING TREAT

PASTELES, ARROZ CON GANDULES, ROAST PORK, PORK CHOPS

GOOD TIME ISLAND MENU FOOD

IN ALL THE CASI ME PEGUÉ BOLITA APARTMENT DWELLINGS

FORCE FED CULTURA ON LA VITROLA

RADIO WADO MINGLED WITH INTOXICATED GROWN-UPS

EXAGGERATING CUENTOS DE LA ISLA

BRINGING TO LIGHT THE PAINFUL

FEELING ASSOCIATED WITH HOMESICKNESS

LA SEPARACIÓN DEL CAMPO Y EL JÍBARO

REUNITED (IN A CROWDED SALA WITH TOO MANY BUTACAS)

BY CORTIJO, DON PEDRO FLORES, DANIEL SANTOS, EL TRÍO
LOS PANCHOS

UNA COLECCIÓN DE MÚSICA CULTURAL

TRANSPORTING OUR PARENTS BACK HOME

ON SCRATCHED-UP SEVENTY-EIGHTS

WHICH EVENTUALLY BECAME HISPANIC FRISBEES

EL SON DE LA LOMA PLAYED ON OUR PHILCO TURNTABLE

THAT WAS ATTACHED TO THE BLACK AND WHITE TV

COVERED WITH A RAINBOW PAINTED TRANSPARENT
PLASTIC

MAKE-BELIEVE COLOR TV

MI ABUELA WOULD WIND ME UP

THEN TURN ME LOOSE ON THE LIVING ROOM FLOOR

UNA PACHANGUITA PARA LA VIEJITA

MY POINTY SHOES WOULD SCRATCH UP THE FLOWER-
COLORED CARPETA

AS I SMOKED A JOHNNY PACHECO TUNE

MY BODY GYRATED TO THE LATIN BEAT

THE PORK AND OTHER GREASE-LADEN PRODUCTS WHICH
WE INHALED

TO COAT OUR CHOLESTEROL STOMACH LININGS

TRADITIONAL FOODS THAT EITHER KILL YOU

OR TURN YOU INTO A JUNKYARD DOG THAT LIVES FOREVER

AGUANTANDO LOS ABUSOS DE LA VIDA

WOULD SHAKE IN ME LIKE A PONCHE IN A HAMILTON BEACH
BLENDER

AS MY GALLITO HAIRDO KEPT ITS PLACE WITH A HEAPING
  HELPING

OF BRILLANTINA ARCA OR WILDROOT OR BOTH

THE CÓMEME LA MENTE YOUNG SISTERS CORO

SINGING THE VEN AQUÍ PAPI SONGS

AS THE MUJERIEGO PARADE OF CHULOS

PACKED THE STORE FRONT SOCIAL CLUBS

THE HOME WRECKERS VS THE HOUSEWIVES

FRIDAY NIGHT GILETTE FIGHTS WERE ALWAYS
  ENTERTAINING

THOSE SWINGING SOUNDS OF THOSE SOCIAL CLUBS

WHICH MY GRANDMOTHER LABELED CORTEJO Y CORTEJA
  GATHERINGS

WOULD ALWAYS CLASH WITH PENTECOSTAL TAMBOURINE
  SOUNDS

WHICH ALSO CLASHED WITH SCHOOL YARD CONGUEROS

WANNABE RUMBEROS

PASSING WINE BOTTLES AND TOOTHPICK JOINTS

CHANTING IN RASPY RHYTHM

"AGUA QUE VA CAER"

VICTOR EL COJO BREAKING EVERYBODY UP WITH HIS
  SPANISH JOKES

TOMÁSO EL NEGRO CUBANO FLIPPING A DOUBLE EDGE
  NAVAJA IN HIS MOUTH

WHILE CHANTING AFRO-CUBAN RELIGIOUS THEMES

NAZARIO SHOWING US ONE HUNDRED WAYS TO USE WIRE
  HANGERS

LOS TRES VIEJOS SINGING A CAPELLA EN SUS GUAYABERAS

FRIDAY NIGHT OFF BROADWAY THEATRE CAME TO US LIVE

ON THE BRONX STREET STAGE

FIRE ESCAPE... ESCAPES... ROOF-TOP STAR GAZING...

TAR BEACH TANNING... ROOF-TOP PHOTO SESSIONS...

ORCHARD BEACH... CONEY ISLAND...

CROTONA PARK FAMILY OUTINGS...

MY FAVORITE ABUELA EUGENIA PERCHED

ON A FIFTH FLOOR WINDOWSILL

WRAPPING LOOSE CHANGE INTO A #2 BAG

THE SLOW MOTION DANCE AS IT PARACHUTED

UNA PESETA INTO MY ANXIOUS HANDS

FOR BONBONS... MARBLES... OR A TOP

AS MY MOTHER WOULD MUMBLE UNDER HER BREATH
    RESPECTFULLY

"QUE ALCAHUETA"

INNER CITY ENTERTAINMENT... HOMEMADE SCOOTERS...
    CARPETA GUNS...

SCHOOL YARD STICK BALL... BOX BALL... PUNCH BALL...
    HAND BALL... CURB

BALL... WE HAD A BALL

EVEN CAUGHT MY PARENTS BALLING IN THEIR BEDROOM
    BALLROOM

GAMES WHICH SOMEHOW TAUGHT US TO BABYSIT
    OURSELVES

DIRECTED OUR UNBRIDLED ENERGY

AND TAUGHT US THE ART OF COMPETITION

CARDBOARD INNERSOLES PROTECTING OUR SOCKS FROM
    CONCRETE

HAND WASHING SOCKS AND STAINED UNDER WEARS

"TIENEN NOVIAS Y NO SABEN LIMPIARSE LAS NALGAS"

EASTER SUITS... CHRISTMAS SUITS... CATHOLIC HOLIDAY
  DEBTS

PAY YOUR LIFE AWAY LAY-AWAYS... DELANCY LEATHER

HOUR-LONG CONSEJOS

WHICH WE WOULD GLADLY TRADE IN

FOR UNOS CUANTOS CHANCLETAZOS

THE IT HURT ME MORE THAN IT HURT YOU BEATINGS

ACCOMPANIED BY A SPOONFUL OF CASTOR OIL

THE DAILY YOU BETTER EAT ALL YOUR BOWLS OF FUNCHE

CORNMEAL OVERDOSE AT AGE SIX

PIGEON COUPS

THOSE WHAT YOU SAY ABOUT MY MOTHER FIGHTS

GO ASK YOUR MOTHER... GO ASK YOUR FATHER...

MERRY GO ROUNDS

DOÑA JUANITA COMPONIENDO SPRAINED ANKLES

LOS SANTEROS SANTIGUERO SESSIONS

RENT PARTIES... HOOKY PARTIES...

THE I DON'T NEED AN EXCUSE TO PARTY PARTIES

RED BULBS GRIND ME UP BLACK AND BLUE THIGH PARTIES

SUNDAY BREAKFAST... FRIED SALAMI... FRIED EGGS...
  ITALIAN BREAD

CHUITO SERENADING US WITH HIS HOMEMADE BOMBAS

"UN VIEJITO Y UNA VIEJITA ESTABAN JUGANDO TROMPO

EL VIEJITO LE DECÍA SI TE PLANTA TE LO ROMPO"

MAKING MY MOTHER BLUSH WITH HIS HEARTFELT BOLEROS

EMPTY BOTTLES OF SEAGRAM SEVEN...

EMPTY BOTTLES OF RHEINGOLD CHUG-A-MUGS

MY X FRIEND MIGUEL SURROUNDED BY #2 BAGS FULL OF
  AIRPLANE GLUE:
  BEHIND P.S. FORTY-TWO

GRACIAS MIS HERMANOS FOR SHARING YOU SOCKS...

BLYE KNITS... PEPPER SILKS... HOPES... FEARS...

BINBASOS... JOINTS AND TEARS

GRACIAS MIS ABUELAS FOR YOUR PASTEL COLORED
  CUENTOS

IN A BLACK AND WHITE WORLD

GRACIAS CHUITO POR ESE SACRIFICIO

PLANCHANDO YOUR LIFE AWAY...

SUDANDO LA GOTA GORDA IN SWEATSHOP CITY

GRACIAS POR ESE AMOR THAT YOU SHARED

WHEN WE LAY SICK IN BED

GIVING US YOUR ATTENTION AND SHOWING YOUR
  CONCERN

QUÉ DIOS LO TENGA BIEN

LA VIEJA CUMPLIÓ NOVENTA Y CINCO

NO MORE MAJA SOAP OR TALCUM POWDER

NO MORE FLUFFY CHANCLETAS TO MATCH HER PINK BATA

CHANCLETAS Y CHANCLETAZOS

LA BENDICIÓN Y UN ABRAZO

ABOUT THE AUTHOR

Riscardo Alvarado a retired union carpenter, is an artesian who conducts workshops teaching children and elders to make miniature masks. Found objects are his medium of choice for creating savvy sculptures to express socio-political statements.

Riscardo also braids two languages—English and Spanish—into thought-provoking verse. He performs his poetry in a cadence uniquely his own. Rumor has it that he makes a finger-lickin' flan (dessert) that, like his poetry, demands coming back for seconds. Mr. Alvarado enjoys traveling, globally. Lessons he learns in his garden keep him connected to inner peace. *Raising A Parent* is his first book.

Made in the USA
Middletown, DE
09 October 2020